1|98

LeRoy Collins Leon County
PUBLIC LIBRARY

*This book has been
presented by
Mrs. LeRoy Collins*

Edison in Florida

University Press of Florida

GAINESVILLE TALLAHASSEE TAMPA BOCA RATON
PENSACOLA ORLANDO MIAMI JACKSONVILLE

Olav Thulesius

Edison in Florida

The Green Laboratory

02 01 00 99 98 97   6 5 4 3 2 1

Library of Congress Cataloging-in-Publication Data
Thulesius, Olav.
Edison in Florida: the green laboratory / Olav Thulesius.
   p. cm.
Includes index.
ISBN 0-8130-1521-9 (alk. paper)
1. Edison, Thomas A. (Thomas Alva), 1847–1931. 2. Edison, Thomas A. (Thomas Alva),
1847–1931—Homes and haunts—Florida. 3. Edison, Thomas A. (Thomas Alva), 1847–
1931—Views on environmental protection. 4. Environmental protection. I. Title.
TK140.E3T55   1997
621.3'092—dc21
[B]   97-6796

The University Press of Florida is the scholarly publishing agency for the State University
System of Florida, comprised of Florida A & M University, Florida Atlantic University,
Florida International University, Florida State University, University of Central Florida,
University of Florida, University of North Florida, University of South Florida, and
University of West Florida.

University Press of Florida
15 Northwest 15th Street
Gainesville, FL 32611

Contents

Introduction

The many biographies of Thomas Alva Edison are mainly about his career as an inventor and his contribution to the development of modern technology.

Edison in Florida considers some lesser-known aspects of the life and thoughts of Edison, the Wizard of Electricity, who made his name in the harsh industrial environment of bustling Yankee towns of North America. Not many people know that the great inventor also lived and worked on the Gulf Coast of Florida. In Seminole Lodge at Fort Myers, he spent the winter months for nearly four decades, far from the smokestacks of the North, in a warm environment, surrounded by subtropical flowers, trees, and animals.

In 1885 Edison chose as his winter home Fort Myers, a settlement in the outback of Florida, a "cow town," difficult to reach and certainly not on the sandy shores of the East Coast that soon would be within easy reach by the rapidly expanding Flagler railroad system. At the time, even Key West, the southernmost outpost of Florida, was more accessible by regular and fast steamboat runs. Edison's choice of Fort Myers might have been the result of a youthful adventure, the search for bamboo (at the time still used as filaments in his electric lamps), and the prospect of bringing a young bride to a balmy paradise. Later, as his family and wealth grew, he could easily have moved to the "Gold Coast" of Florida, such as Palm Beach or Miami, the center of social life and luxury in the state. But Edison stayed in Fort Myers. At heart he still was a country boy longing for a frontier garden in the wilderness; he went his own way and did not follow the crowd.

In Fort Myers he had a laboratory in which he did research. Here he was joined by friends who shared his love of wildlife and camping: the naturalist John Burroughs, the rubber tycoon Harvey Firestone, and his neighbor and greatest admirer, Henry Ford, epitome of industrial mass production but also a bird lover. Mina Miller Edison, his second wife, and his children also visited at Fort Myers.

In this book, I try to explain why the Wizard of Electricity turned to nature, plants, and birds and together with his wife, Mina, and son Theodore became a pioneer of environmental protection. They fought the shameful trade of egrets and parakeets slaughtered for the millinery business. Edison traveled the countryside with his friends, whose prime interest was nature. His interest in nature also led to his last comprehensive research project, the development of rubber from a wayside plant, goldenrod.

Other not so well-known features of the great man are his metaphysical and religious beliefs, as reflected in his interest in the life of sponges he picked up on the shores of the Gulf of Mexico. I also briefly comment on the medical history of the Edison family: the death of his first wife, Mary Stilwell, the deafness of Edison and his son Charles, and his interest in medical issues such as X rays, Polyform liniment, and cures for gout and yellow fever. Hardly anybody knows that Edison was proposed as recipient of the 1915 Nobel Prize and why he never received it.

Edison's winter home in Fort Myers has become the most important monument to the great inventor next to the Edison National Historic Site in West Orange, New Jersey, and the Edison laboratories at Greenfield Village, Dearborn, Michigan. The displays contain a diversity of exhibits, not only including a large collection of technical memorabilia but also a great variety of living tokens from his life such as plants, trees, and flowers.

✳   ✳   ✳

I am grateful to Drs. Reese V. Jenkins, Paul Israel of the Thomas A. Edison Papers at Rutgers University, New Brunswick, New Jersey, and archivist George Tselos at the Edison National Historic Site, West Orange, New Jersey, for helping me in my research. I am indebted for the kind support I received in Fort Myers from Wilbur C. Smith III, mayor of the city of Fort Myers, Robert C. Halgrim, Curator Michele Albion-Wehrwein of the Edison Winter Home, James Newton, Fort Myers Beach, Florida, and Patty Bartlett,

Fort Myers Historical Museum. Special thanks are owed to Leslie Marietta, historian at the Edison Winter Home, for invaluable support throughout the project. For information about the Nobel Prize I am indebted to Anders Bárány, Royal Swedish Academy of Sciences, Stockholm.

My gratitude also goes to Dr. Sven-Göran Fransson, University Hospital, Linköping, Sweden, for providing me with references regarding Edison's X-ray research; Mrs. Jane Nelson, Gorham, Maine, for editing; Cathleen Latendresse, Henry Ford Museum, Dearborn, Michigan, for illustrations; librarians Karen Aust and Lisa Apple, Gulfport Public Library, Gulfport, Florida; and James Strandberg, Firestone Corporation, Akron, Ohio, for providing me with books about Florida and Harvey Firestone.

Finally, my heartfelt thanks go to my wife, Layla, whose continued loving support throughout many years of hardship made this book possible. Because this text covers only some parts of Edison's life and work, a chronology of the most important events in Edison's life is included.

Edison Chronology

1888	Established iron ore milling plant, designed kinetoscope
1889	Developed moving pictures and visited Paris exposition
1894	Opened "peephole" kinetoscope parlor on Broadway
1896	Experimented with X rays
1900	Started development of the nickel-iron-alkaline storage battery; visited Tampa with family
1901	From this year the Edisons regularly spent February and March in Fort Myers
1902	Established a Portland cement plant
1910	Invented the disk phonograph
1914	Edison proposed as a candidate to receive the 1915 Nobel Prize in physics
1915	Visited Luther Burbank in California with Ford and Firestone
1916–24	Took auto camping trips with Ford, Firestone, and Burroughs (Burroughs until 1921)
1923	Started experiments to find a local source of rubber
1926	Planted three hundred Madagascar rubber vines at Fort Myers
1927	Edison, Ford, and Firestone formed the Edison Botanic Research Company of Fort Myers
1929	Eighty-second birthday celebration in Fort Myers with President Herbert Hoover, Henry Ford, and Harvey Firestone as guests; Golden Jubilee of the electric light at Dearborn, Michigan
1931	February 11, eighty-fourth birthday celebration in Fort Myers
1931	Edison died on October 18 at West Orange, New Jersey
1938	Edison Pageant of Light inaugurated in Fort Myers
1947	Mina Edison deeded Seminole Lodge to the city of Fort Myers to be operated as a memorial to Thomas A. Edison
1989	Edison Festival of Light replaced Pageant of Light as the major civic event in Fort Myers
1991	The city of Fort Myers added the former Ford winter home to the Edison complex

How happily situated in this retired spot of earth!
Inspiring with wisdom and valour,
whilst the balmy zephyrs fan him to sleep.

WILLIAM BARTRAM, 1791

 1 Magnet Florida

Florida's Image

As was true for many northerners, Edison first came to Florida for reasons of health. By the 1880s the state had a reputation as a spa because of its mild climate. The Spanish explorer Juan Ponce de Leon searched there for the mystical "Fountain of Youth" in 1513. Later the naturalist William Bartram and John James Audubon of bird fame raved about diaphanous springs of Florida. Purportedly, during the Seminole Wars soldiers and Indians alike took their wounded and sick to a spring to regain their health. These tales were subsequently used in campaigns advertising the attributes of Florida.

Many northerners who came to Florida in search of a cure were asthmatics or consumptives suffering from pulmonary tuberculosis. Warm, dry weather was believed to help cure the disease, and in the absence of any specific treatment, a change of climate was thought to help these sufferers. In Europe they were sent to sanitoriums in the mountains of Switzerland or, if they could afford the journey, to sunny Egypt. In the United States there was a choice of warm southern climates such as Florida and Georgia or the dry climate of Colorado and Minnesota.

Appleton's Illustrated Hand-Book of American Winter Resorts for Tourists and Invalids contained words of praise for Florida: "In addition to the mildness of the climate, the pine forests contribute greatly to its healthfulness. The delicious terebinthine odors exhaled by them not only purify the atmosphere, but impart to it a healing, soothing and peculiarly invigorating quality." The book claimed that the death rate from tuberculosis was more than five times higher in Massachusetts than in Florida. According to *Sea Breeze*, a local newspaper advertising the virtues of Disston City, "We are freer from all kinds of sickness than in any other part of the known world. We are not exempt from death, but life is prolonged to a great length, and there is no cause why a person may not live forever but for the law prohibiting it."[1]

Such reports impressed many invalids, and they came to Florida in ever-increasing numbers. People with chest problems such as the poets Ralph Waldo Emerson and Sidney Lanier went there to seek cures. Even the great Florida railroad pioneers Henry Flagler and Henry Plant first came to Florida because of health problems of their own or of family members.[2]

Ambitious, hardworking, nerve-racked Yankees came to Florida for recreation and to restore their energy.[3] In 1875 Lanier published his *Florida: Its Scenery, Climate and History*, which featured a "Chapter for Consumptives," in which he lyrically concluded: "The question of Florida is a question of an indefinite enlargement of many people's pleasures and of many people's existences as against that universal killing ague of modern life."[4]

A myth was created that Florida was not only a sanitorium for the sick but could even improve people's reproductive vigor. A northern practitioner told childless couples to go to Florida: "A warm climate promises aid in marriages not blessed with offspring. Heat stimulates powerfully the faculty of reproduction!" As early as 1530, Peter Martyr, a writer at the Spanish court, told of an aged man who traveled to Florida: "Attracted by the desire to prolong his life, left to take the longed-for waters of that fountain. He spent some time there, bathing and drinking the waters for many days according to the rules prescribed by the bath attendants. He returned with virile efficacy, acquitted himself in his masculine duties, married again and had children. His son presents as proof of it."[5]

Another writer who promoted Florida was Harriet Beecher Stowe, whose antislavery novel *Uncle Tom's Cabin* had been so influential that Abraham Lincoln called her "the little woman who wrote the book that made this great war." Stowe had acquired a winter home and orange plantation at Mandarin, Florida. In 1873 she wrote: "Florida is particularly adapted to the needs of people who can afford two houses, and want a refuge from the drain that winter makes on the health" and "If I had my say, I wouldn't come north at all. I leave Florida with tears in my eyes."[6]

Questionable Country

Lanier, one of the first promotors of the state, said: "Florida by its very peninsular curve whimsically terminates the United States in an interrogation mark."[7]

Why a question mark? Simply because people did not know enough about the new state. In the early nineteenth century, not everybody agreed that Florida was the Fountain of Youth. Some people praised the healthy climate and lush vegetation, but many warned of pestilential tropical forests and dismal swampland, full of dangers from wild animals, mosquitoes, and disease-carrying fumes. Before the Civil War, the average North American had heard of poisonous swamps and morasses only as described by Daniel Webster in 1851: "No cheerful breezes fan it, no spirit of health visits it. It is all fever and ague. Nothing beautiful or useful grows in it, the traveller through it breathes miasma, and treads among all things unwholesome and loathsome."[8]

This view prevailed during most of the nineteenth century. Americans believed that epidemic diseases such as yellow fever and malaria were caused by "miasma," an infectious air emanating from the decaying matter in swamps and marshes. This opinion was understandable because yellow fever still raged in Florida, with a major outbreak in Tampa and Jacksonville as late as 1888. In addition, people who frequented the swamplands often suffered from malaria.

Hence a dual picture of Florida emerges, one salubrious and attractive and one frightening, replete with dark swamps populated by wild animals. But this exotic aspect probably added to Florida's attraction and was an extra bonus for tourists who were looking for excitement such as shooting alligators from steamers up the Oklawaha River. Both the promise of good weather and health and the lure of dangers of the Florida swamps were advertised in contemporary travel guides.

Rails to Florida

After the Civil War, with booming industrialization and improved communications, Florida became a reality for many who previously had only dreamed about the state. The rapid expansion of railroads made it possible for northerners to travel easily and to make holiday trips. After the war the number of miles in the national railroad network doubled. The period of greatest construction was the decade of the 1880s, when seventy-one thousand miles of new lines were built. Railroad building was most rapid south of the Ohio and Potomac Rivers.[9] From 1880 to 1885 railroad mileage in Florida more than tripled.[10] The west coast of Florida was served by the Plant System, a network of railroads in Georgia, Alabama, and Florida. On the east coast Flagler's Florida East Coast Railway empire expanded south and by 1896 had created the new resort cities of Palm Beach and Miami. In 1912, Flagler's line reached Key West. Fort Myers on the Gulf lagged behind and did not get its own railway connection until 1904 after the Plant System had been purchased by the Atlantic Coast Line.

Edison, the Health Seeker

In January 1879 Edison's oldest son, Tommy, fell ill with a bad cough that developed into bronchitis—at the time a serious problem. The family doctor, Leslie Ward, recommended sending him to Florida to escape the harsh, wet northern climate. Because Edison was busy with the final stages in the development of the electric light bulb, he could not leave from his laboratories in Menlo Park, New Jersey, and the boy's mother, Mary, was too weak to travel after the birth of her second son, Will.

Therefore, it was decided that Alice Stilwell, Mary's sister, should travel with the boy to St. Augustine. Later Mary and the two other children followed. They traveled by train to Savannah, then by steamer to Jacksonville and from there up the St. Johns River. On the way the steamer pulled up at the wharf of Mandarin, famous as the winter residence of Harriet Beecher Stowe. They could see her house, which was on the left side on the shore end of the boat pier. It was a cottage of moderate size, and next to it a magnificent towering tree, a live oak with widespread branches, which gave an air of seclusion and dignity. At Tocoi on the east bank of the St. Johns River they boarded the little Starlight Express for the remaining fourteen miles to St. Augustine. This train was simply a horse-drawn railroad car pulled on wooden rails.

Edison first visited Florida in the winter of 1882, when he spent a month with his ailing wife, Mary, and the children in Green Cove Springs on the St. Johns River. They tried the "sulphur waters of peculiar healing virtues for rheumatism and dyspepsia."[11]

In the winter of 1883–84 Edison and his family again vacationed in St. Augustine. Mary had headaches and bouts of depression, and Thomas suffered from "neuralgia," or nervous tension, because of overwork. He wanted to escape from "the pace that kills." He thought both visits were very beneficial, and the family enjoyed trips up the St. Johns and Oklawaha Rivers, which were becoming tourist attractions. But once recovered from his illness, Edison again became absorbed with problems at work and "fired off letters or telegrams by the hour" from nearby Palatka to his collaborators in New York about the construction of his power station in New York.[12]

This is the female form,
A divine nimbus exhales from it from head to foot,
It attracts with fierce undeniable attraction.

WALT WHITMAN, "I SING THE BODY ELECTRIC"

⇀ 2 ↽   A New Life

In 1884 Thomas Alva Edison's life reached a low ebb. After his immensely successful inventions of the phonograph in 1877 and the electric light bulb in 1879, he encountered enormous problems defending his patent rights and was involved in complicated lawsuits and business transactions. Then there was the battle over whether AC or DC electric current was best, and he was forced to defend his DC electrical power supply against the new "dangerous" AC current. After being an independent inventor who could spend most of his time being creative, he now had to face problems of ligitation and big business.

Tragedy and New Love

In the midst of this turmoil of triumphs and hardship, he experienced a personal tragedy: his wife, Mary, died at the age of twenty-nine, probably as the result of an unidentified disease of the central nervous system ("congestion of the brain," more likely a brain tumor) at their home in Menlo Park, New

Jersey. Officially, the cause of death was said to be typhoid fever, but her previous history of chronic fatigue and headaches makes this very unlikely. Edison was devastated and alone with three motherless children whom he could not properly look after: Marion ("Dot"), twelve, Tom ("Dash"), nine, and Will, seven.

He could not cope with the responsibility and buried himself more and more in his work. The marriage had been problematic. For years Edison had been married to his electrical inventions and spared little time for his family. Although he had provided Mary with all the luxuries of life, he did not understand her personal needs and neglected his children. Mary, a simple soul, jealous of Edison's work and feeling deserted by her husband, must have been unhappy.

At this time he revived his friendship with a former fellow telegrapher, Ezra Torrence Gilliland, who now was head of the Bell Telephone Company's experimental department in Boston. They had worked together in 1864 for Western Union in Ohio. Gilliland was a stout, jovial man, and his wife, Lillian, was a beautiful, extroverted socialite. In an effort to cheer Edison, they introduced him to a succession of eligible young women. One Sunday in the early winter of 1885 he was their dinner guest along with pretty Mina Miller. She was asked to give a recital for the guests and recollected many years later: "I never played for anybody, but they asked me to play, so I thought, oh well, I'll never see these people again, so I played." When asked about Edison, "How did he strike you at the time?" she answered, "Just as a genial, lovely man."[1]

Mina Miller had dark eyes that contrasted with her creamy skin, a mouth whose curves belied her determined chin, and a seductively rounded figure. Mina Miller was only nineteen when she raised her steady gaze to the eyes of the man old enough to be her father. Upon being asked to play, she went at once to the piano and did her best.[2] She and Edison fell in love at first sight. Edison was enchanted by her looks and impressed by her sophisticated and engaging personality. The daughter of a wealthy industrialist and inventor of Akron, Ohio, she moved in the right circles.

Shortly thereafter, Edison went to Chicago on business. There he caught a cold that developed into pneumonia, keeping him in bed in his hotel room for a week. Luckily, the Gillilands were with him, and they called for Marion to come to her father's bedside. After he recovered, Edison decided to make a trip to Florida after attending an exhibition at New Orleans where some of his latest inventions were on display.

Arabian Nights

In February 1885 the weather in St. Augustine was bad, with freezing temperatures. Edison, along with his daughter, Marion, and the Gillilands, stayed at the San Marco Hotel on San Marco Avenue, just outside the city gates, not far from the bay and close to the site of America's oldest town. But Edison was restless. The travel brochures and books praising Florida's climate and its salubrious effect on the sick and convalescents were based on the good winters in northern Florida, around the St. Johns River. Visitors and health seekers were disappointed when they experienced cold winters, however, and were receptive to reports from southern Florida around 1870 praising the frost-free climate of the Keys.

Edison must have studied *Appleton's Illustrated Hand-Book of American Winter Resorts*, which includes a section on the Gulf Coast. Disappointed with the bad weather in St. Augustine, he must have been reassured to read: "A marked difference is seen in this respect between this latitude and that of North Florida. In the latter section the mercury reaches a much higher and a much lower point. This delightful equability of temperature is the great and valuable point to be considered by the invalid who determines to 'go South' for health. Many have had occasion to be thankful for the manifest comfort and extension of life gained by leaving the rude winds of the North for the genial air of the extreme south."[3]

Even Lanier in his guidebook of Florida is enchanted with the west coast:

The tourist and sportsman desiring a mild flavor of adventure, the Gulf coast of Florida offers a charming field; and any invalid who is able to endure the comparative rudeness of this manner of life cannot but find benefit from the liberal air and genial appetites which range together along these quiet shores. There is a certain sense of far-awayness in the wide water-stretches, an indefinable feeling of withdrawal from harsh life, that give to this suave region, as compared to others, the proportion which mild dreams bear to realities. It is a sort of Arabian Nights.[4]

Off to the Gulf

St. Augustine was a great disappointment to Edison: the weather was bad and there were no distractions that interested him. Most other visitors were consumptives who walked slowly along the narrow roads of the old city. For a man of Edison's active spirit who recovered quickly, the scene soon became depressing. He had heard and read about the sunny South of Sidney Lanier and thus was receptive when he met the enterprising L. A. Smith from New York, who raved about the attractions of south Florida, the Gulf of Mexico, and the Keys and suggested that they make a trip down the Gulf Coast. His descriptions of the unusual flora stirred the inquisitive mind of the inventor, who immediately thought of the possibility of finding new sources of natural fibers for his incandescent lamps. Edison quickly decided to set out on an expedition to the south.

Gilliland's wife and Edison's daughter remained in St. Augustine while Edison, Gilliland, and Smith took the train thirty miles to Jacksonville. In this busy town they stayed overnight in the luxurious St. James Hotel before boarding the Florida Transit Railroad. It was a pleasant journey through pine forests, but at Baldwin they changed to a very primitive train to Cedar Keys. Between Gainesville and Bronson their train was derailed three times and they had to spend the night in the uncomfortable compartment on wooden benches. Edison relates the episode thus:

> That railroad was one of the roughest riding affairs I have ever encountered. The trip took three or four days, and during that time we ran off the track at least three times. While we were waiting for the cars to get back on the rails, we had plenty of opportunity to observe the fauna and flora of the State. You may realize just how ordinary a thing it was for the train to run off the track when you learn what the telegraph company did. The Western Union Company, I think, owned the poles that ran alongside the roadbed, and they got tired of having them knocked down by the train, so they took the poles up and placed them farther away from the tracks. Then we cruised around in Florida, and finally reached Fort Myers.[5]

The train entered Cedar Keys across a long bridge that spans a lagoon and rolled slowly through a little yard alongside the freighthouse and station with a boat landing on the opposite side of the track. On the journey, Edison had noticed the big stacks of cedar logs near a factory and machine shop belonging to the Faber brothers, pencil manufacturers of New York, who, like him, also had a business in Newark, New Jersey. They had established a steam sawmill in Florida to produce cedar wood for their lead pencils. The party stayed overnight at Cedar Keys and the next morning chartered the sloop *Jeanette* with Captain Dan Paul, who sailed them down the west coast of Florida to Tampa, then to Sarasota Bay, Charlotte Harbor, and Punta Rassa, where they stopped for a visit.

The *Jeanette* anchored at Punta Rassa, at the mouth of the Caloosahatchee River, and the travelers were kindly received by the jovial, walrus-mustached George Renton Shultz, telegraph operator and hotel manager of the Tarpon House. Edison's attention was immediately aroused by this fellow telegrapher and New Jersey native who had come to Punta Rassa in 1867 when the International Ocean Cable Company established the Cuban telegraph of the Western Union. It was the southernmost link of communication between North America and Cuba and the West Indies. (In 1898 the station carried the news that ignited the Spanish-American War: the sinking of the battleship *Maine* in Havana Harbor.)

Queer Voyage

One legend explains why Edison chose to go upriver to Fort Myers rather than to Key West, the main attraction down the south coast:

> While smoking his cigar under the veranda of the hotel at Punta Rassa, he saw a gentleman and his family putting off in a sloop. It struck him that they were starting a queer voyage, and he asked where they were going. "Up the Caloosahatchee" was the reply. Finding that he could have a glimpse of this unknown stream in a couple of days, he changed his course for Fort Myers, a Rip Van Winkle settlement about twenty miles up the river, on the site of the old forts built to watch the Seminole Indians.[6]

Shultz also must have enticed him to proceed inland because he not only talked business in technical terms of telegraphy but also painted an attractive picture of fishing and of the banks of the Caloosahatchee River and its subtropical vegetation. He described the coconut and date palms, planted by quartermaster Winfield Scott Hancock (later a Civil War general), the breadfruit trees, and the giant Japanese bamboo on Major James Evans's plantation. Carbonized bamboo fibers were the most essential feature of Edison's incandescent lamps, and he was constantly searching for new and better fibers that could be used as lamp filaments.[7] He said: "I want to ransack all the tropical jungles to find a better fibre for my lamps. I expect it to be found in the palms or bamboo."[8]

Edison had instituted a quest for material from which to make a perfectly uniform and homogeneous carbon filament for his incandescent lamps. He carbonized everything in nature he could lay his hands on, from human whiskers to hay. He tried coconut hair, cor, flax, tree shavings, and grass.

To the *New York Times* years later he explained how he finally found the winner. "One hot summer day in 1880 a palmetto fan lying on the table caught my attention and I observed the strip of fiber used to bind the edge. Under a magnifying glass it was seen to have a strong, tough homogeneous body. So we tried carbonizing strips of the fiber and it proved satisfactory." He went on: "Meanwhile, we searched the world for a better fiber. I sent men to South America, the West Indies, and the Far East—throughout the tropical belt—looking for a superior fiber. We tested 6,000 kinds but in the end failed to find any one better than the fiber of my palmetto fan." So Edison sent someone to Japan to obtain a supply of bamboo. That was still the situation when he went to Florida.

Edison was aware that there were many other likely plant fibers in Florida: Spanish moss that hung from the trees and a great variety of palm trees with long fronds. He probably had heard about the blue palmetto praised by W. G. Benedictine, who had obtained a patent for a process using palmetto fibers for mattress filling.[9] If the fronds were good for mattresses, perhaps they would do for lamp filaments.

These were temptations Edison could not resist, and so the party decided to proceed upriver. They anchored at Fort Myers. The little tropical village was so attractive that they were delighted to stay the night at the Keystone Hotel. The following evening they left to go back to Tampa and then took the train to Jacksonville and St. Augustine.

A Winter Home

Edison's journey along the west coast of Florida was more than a curious adventure. He had in mind looking for a winter retreat. And because both Edison and Gilliland were so impressed with the natural beauty of the peaceful village of Fort Myers, they asked the real estate agent J. Huelsenkamp to find a suitable piece of land. Shortly before they left Fort Myers, they were shown a thirteen-acre parcel along the river that had been purchased a few years before by the cattle baron Samuel Summerlin for $500. Edison immediately liked the place and instructed the agent to purchase it if the price was right.

Edison was interested in the property because he wanted to get away from the harsh winters of the North and was impressed by the pleasant weather on the Gulf Coast, the possibility of finding potentially useful plants, good fishing, and the chance to escape from ever more pressing business.

An omnivorous and rapid reader, he studied not only handbooks and travel guides about health spas and recreational trips but also more serious tracts dealing with the settlement of Florida and the state's natural resources and living conditions such as Ledyard Bill's *A Winter in Florida*, with its "observations on the soil, climate and products of our semi-tropical State, together with hints to the tourist, invalid, and sportsman," and George Barbour's guide for tourists and settlers in Florida.[10] Florida had become more than a temporary haven for the sick who went there to regain their health. People were beginning to build winter homes there to avoid the cold, wet northern winters.

The most famous pioneer in this movement was Harriet Beecher Stowe, who in the 1870s had acquired a winter home and orange grove at Mandarin on the St. Johns River. In her book enthusiastically praising Florida, *Palmetto-Leaves*, she writes: "As people now have summer-houses at Nahant or Rye, so they might, at a small expense, have winter-houses in Florida, and come here and be at home. That is the great charm, to be at home. A house here can be simple and inexpensive, and yet very charming. Already, around us a pretty group of winter-houses is rising: and we look forward to the time when there will be many more."[11]

Hence in 1885 Florida offered Edison the possibility of a winter haven for relaxation, fishing, plant research, and undisturbed work. As he wrote: "I looked forward to the time when I would be getting on in years and would want to come to Florida every winter, and I couldn't imagine a nicer place than Fort Myers. There were wild ducks by the acre, the river was full of fish, and it seemed to afford a perfect opportunity for rest and recreation."[12]

The book of Nature here is never shut
and clasped with ice and snow as in the North.

HARRIET BEECHER STOWE, *Palmetto-Leaves*

$\rightarrow$ 3 $\leftarrow$ Fort Myers

Fort Myers began as a lonely army outpost used for shipping out unwanted
Indians during the Seminole Indian Wars. During the Civil War it was used
as a Union cattle depot. The fort was abandoned after each war was over.

Frontier Settlement

Civilian settlement began in 1866 when the Spanish-American sailor Manuel
Gonzalez and his family moved up from Key West to live in the ruins of the
abandoned fort. Other pioneers were Major James Evans (who had planted
the bamboo that impressed Edison) and Captain Francis Hendry, both of
whom decided to settle on the banks of the Caloosahatchee River and enter
the cattle business after quitting military service. After the Civil War, nearby
Punta Rassa, the former Fort Denaud, where the water was deep close to the
shore at the mouth of the river, became the cattle trading center of south
Florida. The boom started when in Havana the Spaniards, cut off from their
own supplies by local rebels, bought cattle to feed their soldiers from Florida

traders and paid with shining gold doubloons.

Nevertheless, the people of the little southern frontier settlement were painfully aware of the "notorious fact that their town was insignificant" and hardly known only fifty miles away. Therefore, they tried hard to promote its special advantages. Among other things, they desperately wanted a newspaper to tell the world of their existence. In 1884, when New York news editor Stafford Cleveland (a relative of President Grover Cleveland) was bringing his printing press south to Fort Ogden by the Peace River, the captain of the schooner carrying Cleveland brought him to Fort Myers instead. There the promoters of the future town rushed to the dock and convinced Cleveland that Fort Myers "was the place to settle down, set up his newspaper plant, and become rich and influential."[1] Lucky for Fort Myers, Cleveland agreed and set up his business there!

Edison's Eden

When in March of 1885 Edison and his party sailed from Punta Rassa up the Caloosahatchee River, Fort Myers was a primitive frontier settlement. It was not even an incorporated town. But it had a post office, stores, and Cleveland's newspaper, the *Fort Myers Press*, which had begun a publicity campaign extolling the area's mild, frost-free weather: "The Caloosahatchee, a stream rivalling the St. John's in romance, grandeur and beauty, at this point makes a graceful curve, similar to that in the St. John's opposite Palatka, disclosing on its southern bank the city of Fort Myers." Before the arrival of the Edison party, the *Press* wrote:

> For invalids Fort Myers offers advantages unequaled at any point in Florida. Its mild, bracing atmosphere tones up the system and sends the glow of health to the cheeks. To the tourist the wild, varying scenery of the tropics, interspersed with visions of grazing cattle and traces of civilization, affords much enjoyment. To the sportsman the forests teeming with game and river abounding with fish, while the alligators, bears and wild cats can easily be reached in a day, makes this spot a veritable "Hunters' Elysium." We claim this to be not only the Eden of Florida but this part of America.[2]

Edison probably never read these enticing news items in the *Fort Myers Press*, but editor Cleveland, who had experienced northern weather, tried to attract people and knew he had a scoop when he heard the rumors about Edison's plans. He immediately reported:

They were much pleased with the Caloosahatchee and with Fort Myers; and Mr. Edison is negotiating for the purchase of a good location here. If he buys a place, he says he will fit it up handsomely and make it a pleasant abode, if such a thing is possible. He will also bring along a forty-horsepower steam engine and set up his workshop and laboratory, for a portion of the year. The people of Fort Myers are highly pleased at the prospect of such a distinguished addition to their community.[3]

Edison immediately fell in love with the tropical bower on the banks of the big river. Here he found what he had longed for: a frost-free, warm climate and the very private atmosphere of a peaceful village where he hoped to be undisturbed. The prime attraction, no doubt, was the vast, unspoiled wilderness and lush vegetation, but Edison was also intrigued by the bamboo bushes at the waterfront of Major Evans's plantation and the Vivas place.[4] (Bamboo was the source of the carbon filament used in Edison's incandescent lamps.) Bamboo was originally introduced to Florida from Japan with a consignment of orange trees, and it gradually spread over the entire Gulf Coast.

A Bold Venture

A week after Edison's arrival, on March 28, 1885, the *Fort Myers Press* jubilantly announced: "Thomas A. Edison is to have the Summerlin place just at the bend of the river about one mile from the business center of Fort Myers. It embraces thirteen acres of land and it is a location of decided natural beauty. He does not, as we understand, propose to wait long before making a commencement."[5]

Edison had a vision. He was so enthralled by thoughts of the future that the incredible story he had told Heulsenkamp was leaked through the *Press* to the astonished village people: he would not only build two houses but also a laboratory, and he would bring a steam engine and an electric power plant.

Edison gladly paid $2,850 for the property and was convinced that he had made a good deal. The purchase was a joint venture with his friend and associate Ezra Gilliland, who owned a 25 percent share of the property. Even before the purchase was finalized, Edison had in mind plans for the winter homes, one for himself and the other for the Gillilands, and nearby a space for a private laboratory.

Honeymoon

Edison had fallen in love with Mina Miller, who was decribed as being "beautiful, for she has one of the sweetest faces that a human being is blessed with. In her manner she is queenly, and is an exceptionally handsome and brilliant lady." His thoughts of the future revolved around the prospect of marriage to Mina, and during a brief period in July 1885 he kept a diary expressing his feelings. He wanted to create a winter haven where he could bring his future wife and have her all to himself. He fancied himself sitting on the porch of a lovely home looking out on the palm-lined river. He described in detail the modern amenities with which he would to equip the houses he planned for himself and his friend Ezra Gilliland, whom he called Damon. In a lyrical moment Edison described his feelings:

> Damon and I, after his return, study plans for our Floridian bower in the lowlands of the pensinsular Eden, within that charmed zone of beauty, where wafted from the table lands of the Oronoco and the dark Carib Sea, perfumed zephyrs forever kiss the gorgeous flora. Rats! Damon promised to ascertain probable cost chartering schooner to plough the Spanish main loaded with our hen coops.
>
> Constantly talking about Mina, whom Damon and I use as a yardstick for measuring perfection. Saw a lady who looked like Mina. Got thinking about Mina and came near being run over by a street car. If Mina interferes much more will have to take out an accident policy.[6]

After a short and intense courtship they were engaged in August 1885 and married in February the following year.

From Dream to Reality

Drawing up plans was one thing, but realizing them in the wilderness of Fort Myers was another. The perfectionist Edison had high expectations, and he laid out his Elysium in Florida in great detail. In Fort Myers Edison employed Colonel J. P. Perkins to make a survey and a diagram of the waterfront property. Edison had drawings of the proposed houses made and ordered prefabricated components of the buildings to be assembled by the Kennebec Framing Company in Fairfield, Maine, and ultimately erected on the spot. The Edison and Gilliland houses were among the first prefabricated homes in America.[7]

The ready-made walls were to be loaded on board a ship at Boston, which would stop at New York to take on board boilers, steam engine, machinery, and other equipment for the laboratory and furniture for shipment to Florida. The cargo was properly insured. Before making these orders, he had telegraphed Perkins in Fort Myers to get exact details about the depth of water in the Caloosahatchee River at high and low tide to ensure undisturbed transport. From this information he learned that the ship had to unload at the mouth of the river in Punta Rassa and that a barge drawing no more than three and a half feet of water would be needed to reach the final destination. Therefore, the cargo also included a steam launch and a lighter.

The first construction planned was a pier reaching far enough into the river so that the launch bringing in building material and supplies from Punta Rassa could tie up. In his final letter to Perkins he wrote:

> We are unable to procure vessels sufficiently light in draught to go up the river. We would like to have ascertain what arrangements can be made for unloading the ship at Punta Rassa and necessary storage room for furniture and such material as cannot be exposed to the weather during the time the buildings are being erected. We will send three or four employees to superintend the work. They will probably require assistance in hauling the material as well as in construction of the buildings. Will probably need four carpenters and four laborers, can they be obtained at Fort Myers?[8]

The *Fort Myers Press* eagerly followed each step of the project and reported on the progress: "EDISON is coming. Work is rapidly progressing on the place under the skillful direction of his capable agent, Eli Thompson, but at the present rate of progress Fort Myers will be ready for electric lights and street railways before the winter is over."[9] Such a bold suggestion aroused doubt even in the minds of the most optimistic people in town that such a fantastic project would be realized. The inhabitants of Fort Myers were eagerly awaiting the arrival of the great man.

On January 9, 1886, three members of Edison's construction team arrived, but the ship with its valuable cargo of building material was not there yet. The people of Fort Myers became impatient: "Slowly but surely the men for Mr. Edison's work are gathering at Fort Myers, and upon the arrival of his schooner operations will commence in full blast." A week later, the schooner finally showed up, and on February 13 the *Fort Myers Press* reported: "Two of Edison's buildings have been erected. We regret to learn that a 200 ton schooner belonging to Mr. T. A. Edison, loaded with material for his laboratory at his place, has gone ashore somewhere on the east coast. We understand, however, that he has ordered the cargo duplicated and will at once ship the same." The lost cargo probably included not only machinery and building material for the laboratory but also the prefabricated houses.[10]

Edison spared no money in completing the building project and even employed a landscape gardener from Philadelphia, who "laid out the place in splendid shape and set out with various kinds of trees and plants, which when they have attained their growth, will greatly add to the beauty of this already favored spot. There are limes, lemons, coconuts, etc. and at the entrance he has placed Spanish bayonets of graded sizes, the trunks of which he has neatly trimmed." The *Fort Myers Press* reporter noted: "The road [to the Edison place] is being worn, he should judge that many of our citizens are more or less interested in that direction. A few weeks ago, as we wended our way down the river, very few improvements were noticeable on the place, but today all is changed, buildings and other improvements having sprung up with a rapidity that rivals the growth of the mushroom." "The houses are two story buildings, square roofed, with a broad piazza running around three sides, while a large kitchen is attached to both. Wires are also being put in that the buildings may be lighted by electricity." The *Press*, promoter of the year-round warm weather in Fort Myers, pointed out: "Dictated by good common sense, Mr. Edison has had a large fireplace built in each house, thus providing against chilly weather which even this area of South Florida is subject to during months of December and January. This is something we would urge upon all who contemplate building anywhere in the State."[11]

Here Comes the Bride

On February 27, 1886, the *Fort Myers Press* announced the arrival of the Gillilands and Edison's daughter Marion with two maids and commented proudly: "When Mr Edison arrives with his newly made wife, Fort Myers can laugh at her neighbors and defy competition." There were rumors that a reception or parade would be held to honor Edison and his bride, but "we understand that he is strongly opposed to such proceedings. We have heard it mentioned that it would be much more acceptable to him for our people to make a sixty foot avenue from our city to his place on the Caloosahatchee. It would not cost more than $100, a good part of the job already completed. Let something be done in this direction."[12]

The same edition of the *Press* contained a long article about the Edison wedding in Ohio. A March 20, 1886, headline read: "HURRAH FOR THOMAS A. EDISON." When Edison and his bride arrived on the little steamer *Manatee* from Tampa, the houses were not quite ready, and the honeymooners had to spend the first part of their stay at the Keystone Hotel on First Street, which was built on stilts over the river. When they finally moved to their own home, they were given a musical welcome by the newly formed Fort Myers Brass Band in its first public appearance. Mina Edison later said she had never before heard such "ethereal" music.[13]

The newlyweds were not left alone. The Gillilands and Edison's daughter had arrived in February, and they also stayed in the Keystone Hotel, where in April they were joined by Mr. and Mrs. Lewis Miller, the parents of the bride.

The couple had hardly settled when Edison's staff in New Jersey began to flood him with telegrams and letters. One complained: "We have not heard a word from him. It is three weeks since he married and he has taken no notice whatever of us in all that time. We have written to him, we have telegraphed him. We get no response. He has cut us dead. We ask him questions requiring immediate attention and that is the last of it. We are running the concern without him. He ignores the telegraph and despises the mail."[14]

When in May the parties finally left Fort Myers, it was rumored that Mina was pregnant.

The Big Attraction

In February 1887 Thomas Edison and the Gillilands returned to Fort Myers. Mina stayed behind in West Orange, New Jersey, because she was in a late stage of pregnancy. Edison had looked forward to the trip because he was recovering from a severe chest infection and needed the balmy weather of Florida and a well-deserved rest from the stressful business activities in New Jersey and New York.

Up north he was constantly haunted by newspaper reporters. In Fort Myers he hoped to be left alone but not so. Rumors had it that the great inventor was overworked and seriously ill and had fled to avoid the demands of work. A reporter for the *New York World*, Sidney Smith, hoping to find a good story, decided to travel to Florida in March. He took the train to Punta Gorda, then the terminus of the Florida Southern Railroad, and while on board the little steamer that carried him through Charlotte Harbor up the Caloosahatchee River he wrote: "Thomas Edison, the famous electrician, was so enraptured with the natural beauty of the area that he at once made up his mind to settle in what fashionable people call the oblivion of still life." He went on: "Much has been said lately of the physical infirmities of the famous electrician that we had expected to meet a man dying slowly but surely in the agonies of consumption." After arriving in Fort Myers he recorded the following conversation:

"I understand from some reports that you have been compelled to seek rest and forego your electrical researches for the present?" nervously queried the reporter.

"Rest! Why, I have come down here to work harder, if anything. I will tell you how I rest: I am working on at least six or seven ideas. When I get tired of one I switch off to another and alternate to such an extent that I have a constant succession of new and pleasurable efforts."

"But don't you get confused in that manner?"

"Not in the least. On the contrary, when working on one idea I often drop in something helping another idea, because they mostly tend to one grand result."

"Don't you feel any effects of your past sickness?"

"Why I can't say that I do, unless this is one," and the electrician bared an arm, showing an ugly little sore.

"What is that?" asked the reporter.

"Oh, nothing much. When administering an injection during my sickness the syringe probably struck a nerve, and this is the result, but it is healing rapidly."[15]

Electric Laboratory

A forty-horsepower steam engine, dynamo, and experimental equipment had been shipped to Fort Myers to complete the laboratory that had been started the year before. The original laboratory building was erected on the riverside and looked like a big steam locomotive. It had a boiler house, a cistern on the roof, and was topped by a fat chimney. Inside at the back was the place for the steam engine and dynamo, the "Long-waisted Mary Ann," as well as the laboratory with benches, tools, and hundreds of bottles. At the entrance was the "thinking room" with a cot where Edison could take catnaps.

The citizens of Fort Myers were enthralled on March 27, 1887, when the lights were turned on for everybody to see and "almost everyone in town wandered out to Edison's home that evening to witness the miracle of science."[16] It is tempting to think this was the debut of electricity in Florida, but in 1883 Edison lights had been installed in the luxurious St. James Hotel in Jacksonville—eight outlets in the lobby and eight outside. Before the turn of the century only enterprising businessmen installed small electric units for their own use. Municipal plants were built only at the turn of the century.[17]

A Clash

After his early enthusiasm, Edison lost interest in his Florida home, and he did not visit Fort Myers between 1888 and 1901. During these years, he was extremely busy with new projects and business ventures, especially a big iron ore project in Ogden, New Jersey, and the development of the cinematoscope. To make matters worse, he had a serious clash with Ezra Gilliland, who had betrayed him in business related to the marketing of his phonograph. As a result, Edison advised the groundkeeper in Fort Myers that he wanted nothing to do with the Gilliland property, which was put up for sale. In 1892 the Gilliland part of the estate was sold to Ambrose M. McGregor, a millionaire oil magnate and associate of John D. Rockefeller. He renamed the cottage Poinciana.

Mina Edison would have liked to go south to relax and in hopes of having her husband to herself (he was away from home most of the time), but after the first visit she gave birth to three children, Madeleine, Charles, and Theodore, born in 1888, 1890, and 1898, and was afraid to make the journey, which was difficult even after 1887, when the Florida Southern train connection was established to Punta Gorda. Schedules on this line were not met, and when the train stopped for fuel or water, trainmen and passengers might wander off into the woods and cowboys liked to shoot at the swinging kerosene lamps of the train. There was also a yellow fever scare, and in May 1887 George R. Shultz, the telegraph operator and health officer of the Fort Myers district, issued a forty-day quarantine "against Key West and any other place infected with yellow fewer."[18] The following year there was a serious yellow fever epidemic in Jacksonville and Tampa. In addition, there was the constant fear of malaria.

During this difficult period, Edison asked his father, Samuel, to look after his Florida home, and when Samuel died in 1896, Thomas decided to put the property up for sale the following year, asking $6,000 for the buildings alone and $7,500 if the machinery was included.[19] Because of the special design of the house, however, and the big laboratory, no buyer could be found and Edison rented the house to Daniel Floweree of Montana.

By the end of the century Fort Myers was starved for news about Edison. The most exciting event happened in February 1898, when Edison's twenty-two-year-old son Thomas came to town. The *Fort Myers Press* reported:

THE YOUNG WIZARD IS HERE. Mr. Thomas A. Edison jr, son of the great inventor and Mr. J. Henry Gill (a friend), of Orange New Jersey, are taking a much needed rest from their laborious work in developing new electrical and other appliances. Young Edison doesn't travel on the reputation of being "his father's son," for he is making a name of his own that promises to be as well known throughout the world as is that of the great Wizard today. In fact the young fellow pulled out of his father's business five months ago and is now going it on his own hook.

The young man's projects were described:

Already he has startled the scientific world with some inventions he is now at work on. He informs us that he is having patented a new chemical film for incandescent light, and that will give more powerful light than present incandescent lights. Another of his new ideas is an aerial ship. He succeeded in floating an air ship 10 feet long, rigged up after the manner of a sailing vessel, with masts, but instead of ordinary sails he used sails inflated with gas; the air ship was also supplied with a center board, etc. He has not followed this up as he is too busy with other ideas.

When asked whether he had invented an instrument for photographing thought he demurred, saying that the papers had made more of this rumor than the facts warranted.[20]

Thomas Jr. was a disturbed young man who suffered from a lack of attention from his father and who could not live up to his expectations. He, however, could speak as convincingly of future inventions as Edison himself and clearly had delusions of grandeur about his own potential inventive prowess. His New York physician had advised him to go south to improve his health.[21]

Finally, in 1900 Edison decided to spend the winter in Fort Myers. The move was planned for January, but that was not possible because his own house was still occupied by Floweree, who was awaiting the completion of his own new magnificent house in Georgian revival style on the riverfront.[22] In March Edison became restless. He had to go to Florida. The family arrived in Tampa on March 5 and stayed at the comfortable new Tampa Bay Hotel.

"What the heck is that," a startled Edison exclaimed when he first saw the silver Moorish minarets and turrets of the palatial Tampa Bay Hotel. The family was met at the train by a friend. No luxury was spared, but Edison did not feel comfortable at the hotel. He went to see cigar manufacturing establishments while the children enjoyed the rickshaws, swimming pool, and dog kennels. Edison, however, discovered the electric hotel launch *Branford* and rode up the Hillsborough River observing alligators sunning on the riverbanks and mullets jumping.

The *Tampa Tribune* reported: "The electrical wizard of the present century is stopping at the Tampa Bay Hotel. Mr. Edison is an affable gentleman, with a mild and pleasant face, short, rather stout in build." The reporters were eager to get the latest news on his inventions and gossip about big business up north, but Edison waved and said: "I am not in Florida for business, but merely for the health of myself and my family. Mrs Edison accompanies me as well as our two children [obviously the youngest, Theodore, was left with his nanny in West Orange]. My intention in coming to Florida is merely for pleasure, and to escape the rigors of the winter at home."[23]

Transportation connections to Fort Myers were still difficult, but Edison decided he wanted to take the train to Kissimmee and from there a paddle wheeler through Lake Okeechobee down the Caloo-sahatchee River. This plan did not work out. His boat, the *Hamilton Disston*, got stuck in the shallows near Southport and he had to return by a northbound steamer and take the train.[24]

There is a state in Dixieland
where breezes softly blow,
where golden orange citrus bloom
where ferns and palm trees grow.

HENRY RESTORFF (DIRECTOR OF EDISON BAND),
FROM "FLORIDA, MY FLORIDA"

 **4** **Seminole Lodge**

By the time Edison came to Florida, most people did not know much about the few remaining Indians who had been driven to the remote swamps of the Everglades. Nevertheless, Edison decided to call his winter home Seminole Lodge after the original inhabitants of Florida, the Seminoles, the only American Indians who have never been conquered and subdued by Uncle Sam.

Florida Indians

The Edisons liked the Seminoles they occasionally saw in Fort Myers and when making tours upriver and in the swamps. At that time both male and female Indians still wore the full tribal costume with wide tunics or great skirts. The children were usually dressed like their parents, in miniature. Edison and particularly his wife, Mina, were impressed by their colorful dresses and found them polite, honest, and stoic in the face of adversity. They felt sympathy for these people of Florida who for centuries had been persecuted and robbed of all their possessions.

When in the nineteenth century Florida was being settled, the Indians were declared outlaws and systematically hunted down. The official opinion was that they were savages, and judgment about them in the 1850s was influenced by the government and some early settlers who had suffered from Indian raids. Washington tried to solve the problem by deporting them, and in 1853 Congress passed an act decreeing that "it shall be unlawful for any Indian or Indians to remain within the limits of the State, and that any Indian or Indians that may remain, or may be found within the limits of this State, shall be captured and sent west of the Mississippi."[1] Edison's sympathy for the Seminoles led him to name his house after them.

Winter Haven

After 1901 Seminole Lodge again became the winter haven for the Edison family, and when they returned on February 27 of that year, Captain Gonzales flew all the flags on his steamer, the *H. B. Plant*, in honor of his distinguished passengers. Three new members of the family joined them: Madeleine, Charles, and the baby Theodore. On arrival, when interviewed by the *Fort Myers Press*, Edison promised to come back every year. He had decided not to sell Seminole Lodge but to improve the property, rebuilding the dock and modernizing the laboratory. He engaged Harvey Heitman as caretaker and Ewald Stulpner, an expert horticulturist, to look after the gardens. He drilled an artesian well, flooding a stream thirty feet aboveground. In 1905 he installed a new electrical plant to supply power to the houses and laboratory.

In 1906 Edison was able to buy the adjacent Gilliland winter home. Before he purchased it, the property had changed hands twice: first it was acquired by Ambrose McGregor and then by R. I. Travers. Edison made the major renovations which are still in place today, transforming it into a guest house with adjoining kitchen.[2]

The extended Seminole Lodge became the meeting place for the family and guests. Charles Edison remembered:

> For a number of years when I was a child mother and father didn't go to Florida at all during the winter. One year they did. I must have been about eight or ten, because I was still wearing short pants and sailor suits. A great deal of the excitement of my youth was centered in and around Fort Myers. Father spent a great deal of time importing exotic plants and trees from tropical climes all over the world. He also kept pretty busy in the laboratory he had built. But mostly it was relaxation. He enjoyed the life down there, as did the family. We had a good many

visitors; people like John Burroughs, the naturalist, Henry Ford and his family, the Firestones, and many others.

Our property had a dock that ran out to deep water in the channel of the Caloosahatchee. The dock was just under a quarter mile long. There was a big summer house at the end. We also had a swimming pool. So it was a wonderful spot to be. I thoroughly enjoyed it, and father truly loved the place. He'd go fishing off the dock or in a boat. He always used to say that fishing was the greatest relaxation he knew of, because "there's something about that line down in the water that forbids anything to enter your mind except the nibble you might get." He used to fish for complete mental relaxation.[3]

Of all the Edison children Charles had especially good memories about Seminole Lodge because in March 1918 he married Carolyn Hawkins there under the tropical foliage of the garden. The wedding took place with only Mina Edison present. Charles's father, chairman of the Naval Consulting Board, was on war duty off Key West and could not come. He sent a cable from his warship: "If it's going to be, then the sooner the better. Anyway, it won't be worse than life in the front-line trenches. You have my blessings."[4]

During the war Edison created forty-two marine warfare devices, including a submarine sonar, a torpedo-obstructing net, an air detection system, underwater searchlights, and night glasses.

Water Jaunts

For the Edison family Florida held many attractions: the balmy weather, unusual flowers, trees, and animals, and the adventure of excursions on land and water.

At the turn of the century, when Edison made Seminole Lodge his winter home, the streets of Fort Myers were made of crushed shells, and when strolling at night it was well to stay in the center so as not to stumble over cows sleeping on the side paths. Sandy wagon ruts outside town made inland excursions difficult and dangerous even if palmetto leaves were laid on the mud, a custom advocated by the locals.[5]

The Edisons occasionally used a horse and buggy, but the most convenient way to travel was by boat. Next to the pier Edison built a boathouse for five rowboats and a naphta launch, the *Mina*. In 1904, having perfected his storage batteries, he added the *Reliance*, a large electric launch that was his favorite sea craft. Initially the batteries had to be charged at the Seminole Power and Ice Company's plant because the electrical equipment in his own laboratory was outmoded.[6]

Before the advent of motor cars, the favorite pastime was boat trips up the winding Caloosahatchee River to the mysterious waters of Lake Okeechobee or Twelve Mile Creek (now Orange River) or seaward to San Carlos Bay and the barrier islands Sanibel and Captiva. Another pleasure was fishing off the pier or from the *Reliance*. Mina and the children were especially fond of the silvery island beaches. If they did not rent a steamer for an extended trip, they could drive to the landing of the Kinzie steamers at the foot of Jackson Street, where they boarded the handsomely equipped *Gladys* bound for the twin islands. On these trips there was much to see: jumping fish, the fins of dolphins, and pelicans gliding through the air and occasionally plunging abruptly into the sea. Sanibel had exceptional attractions: favorable currents deposited thousands of shells on the shining white sand. In addition, the islands were a bird lover's paradise, with beautiful waterfowl and rich vegetation of mangrove jungles offering magnificent roosting places for ibises, roseate spoonbills, and the frigate bird, the supreme flyer that soared at great heights over the Gulf waters and was especially impressive during the breeding season, when its throat swelled into a crimson balloon to attract a partner.

On Sanibel the Edisons sometimes stayed the night at Harriet Matthew's Island Inn. On the island Edison had become friends with Henry Shanahan, the lighthouse keeper, whose eight children roamed the beaches. They were a jolly lot who liked music and dancing. Edison once surprised them with a present: a phonograph and plenty of rolls of recorded music. The Shanahan boys were eager guides, showing the Edisons around the beaches and helping find the best shells to fill their buckets. It came as a surprise when the lighthouse keeper told them that the conches are fiercely carnivorous and feed on fellow molluscs by penetrating their shells with their teeth. After a bridge was built over Blind Pass to the adjacent Captiva Island, Clarence Rutland, a relative of the Shanahans, brought a Model T Ford and offered to meet passengers at the landing and taxi them on a jolting ride over the islands.[7]

Sometimes the Edisons took boat trips to St. James City on Pine Island or went all the way to Punta Gorda to stay at the fashionable resort hotel there that was frequented by tarpon-fishing enthusiasts from up north such as the Vanderbilts.

Wet-Tail Boats

In the 1880s, when Edison appeared on the scene, the hot issue in south Florida was water—water and grass. A rich toolmaker from Philadelphia, Hamilton Disston, saw a great future in the wetlands of the Everglades. His vision was to transform this immense river of grass into fertile farmland. He bought four million acres from the Florida Internal Improvement Fund at the ridiculous price of twenty-five cents an acre. He reasoned that if he could tap the water table of big Lake Okeechobee by digging drainage canals to the Atlantic Ocean and the Gulf of Mexico, he could suck out the wetness from the Kissimmee region. The only natural drainage of the lake was the shallow, winding Caloosahatchee River, with bottlenecks above Fort Thompson at Lake Flirt and Hicpochie. By deepening the riverbed at these sites, Disston hoped to pull the plug from the reservoir of Lake Okeechobee, thereby lowering the water table. The ambitious project brought dredges, steamboats, and skippers to Fort Myers. These boats were low-draft stern-wheelers, which folks jokingly called "wet-ass" or "wet-tail" boats.[8] Edison loved these steamers and became friendly with the Menge brothers, who later owned most of them.

In 1888, after the Disston project to drain the Everglades was suspended, Fred Menge, an engineer on one of the dredges, purchased two small steamers from the company and began offering upriver transportation service to the public. It became an immediate success and later was expanded to become the Menge Brothers Steamboat Line, when Fred's brother Conrad joined as a partner. They soon added larger and more commodious stern-wheelers such as the *Suwanee* and the *Thomas A. Edison* to the fleet. The *Thomas A. Edison* became the pride of the steamboat line. Built in 1901, it was a sleek, 80-foot stern-wheeler, 20.5 feet wide, that had two decks with eleven staterooms and a 9-by-11-foot dining room on the upper deck and space for transport of orange boxes on the lower deck. The boat was purchased for the upriver Caloosahatchee run but was also used twice a week by the Plant System's shuttle service between Punta Gorda and Fort Myers via the island landings in Charlotte Harbor until 1904, when the Atlantic Coast Line established a rail connection to Fort Myers. The Edisons occasionally chartered the *Edison* for trips to Sanibel. Sadly, in 1914 it was destroyed by fire.[9] According to the old Okeechobee skipper Lawrence Will:

> I reckon that the finest of all their boats were the passenger packet THOMAS A. EDISON. She'd been built at Apalachicola, drawed only

2 1/2 feet light, and besides her passengers, could haul 1200 boxes of oranges. She were a beauty of a boat, but she come to a right sad end. On the night of January 30, 1914, with a full load of fruit, she were tied up at Lee County Packing House. That were the night when the packin' house ketched afire, and hit some of the neighborin' buildings burned slap to the ground. The same wind which fanned the fire had lowered the river. The EDISON were hard and fast aground and all the tugboats couldn't budge her a-loose, and that were the last of the THOMAS A. EDISON.[10]

Edison was fond of boat trips to the barrier islands, but his favorite jaunts were up the peaceful Caloosahatchee. At the time the river was a pretty sight. There were no bridges or locks to obstruct the sail. With great interest, he observed life on the river. He saw citrus groves, sugarcane, pineries, and the landings of little villages and settlements bearing such euphonious names as Olga, Rialto, Caloosa, Ovanita, Alva, and LaBelle, adding to the charm of the trip along this lovely stream. He watched the loading of boxes of citrus and pineapples and delivery of passengers, animals, barrels, and hampers. Farmers forded their long-horned cattle across shallow waters at marshy grounds. The banks were lined with live oaks, cabbage palms, and cypress trees with curtains of moss hanging from their branches. Edison could not hear the steamboat's whistle or the bells, but he felt the throb of the steam engine and paddle wheel, and he could smell the fragrance of tropical flowers near Alva, where there were three solid miles of orange groves loaded with yellow fruit. Upriver in February the scenery was wild: swamp oaks and the pale gray ghost skeletons of bald cypresses, heavy with swaying moss scarves and air plants, sabal palms, and finally the silent mystery of the Everglades with its endless stretches of sawgrass. In the Everglades he could smell the brown Ocheechobee water. He observed a great variety of birds, including snowy egrets, their plumes tossed by the wind, that rose like snowflakes from the shores.

The opening of the North New River Canal from Lake Okeechobee to Fort Lauderdale made it possible to reach the Atlantic Ocean from the Gulf. On April 25, 1912, Governor Albert Gilchrist inaugurated the service. He took the side-wheeler *Thomas A. Edison* from Fort Myers to LaBelle. There the party switched to the smaller *Queen of the Glades*, which reached Fort Lauderdale the following day after a stopover at Ritta on the south shore of Lake Okeechobee.[11]

The *Suwanee* was Edison's favorite steamer for traveling to the East Coast. It was seventy feet long and had ten staterooms on the upper deck and an excellent salon. A promotional leaflet proclaimed: "This service can not be described. It is beyond description. The beauties are untold. The wild bird and game life has not been mentioned. The hunting is the best in the Union. The Seminole still lurks in the forests abounding this route. It is a wilderness for two hundred miles from Gulf to Ocean. No where else in America can such scenes be viewed except from the deck of the steamer SUWANEE.[12]

Edison regularly chartered the *Suwanee* for a trip across the lake. An old skipper who knew him wrote: "On these trips Edison loved to fish, but more'en likely whilst his friends was off a-huntin' deer and turkeys in the hammocks, Edison might be a settin' thar on deck, adreamin' up some new invention."[13]

The *Suwanee* made the cross-country trip in three days. Eventually silting and water hyacinths put an end to these joyful trips, and the boat was destroyed in the 1926 hurricane.[14] The rebuilt steamer is now a museum piece at Henry Ford's Greenfield Village in Dearborn, Michigan.

Why Fort Myers?

When Edison left St. Augustine and went to south Florida, he might have had feelings similar to those of John James Audubon, who half a century earlier, when disappointed at Spring Garden in northeast Florida, exclaimed: "Here I am in the Floridas, thought I, a country that received its name from the odours wafted from the orange groves, to the boats of the first discoverers, and which from my childhood I have consecrated in my imagination as the garden of the United States. A garden where all that is not mud, mud, mud, is sand, sand, sand. These things had a tendency to depress me, notwithstanding some beautiful flowers, rich looking fruit, a pure sky, and ample sheets of water at my feet." Audubon's opinion changed drastically, however, when he came to south Florida. His heart "swelled with uncontrollable delight" when he reached Indian Key and Cape Sable in the Gulf of Mexico.[15] The two men had different quests: Audubon was chasing birds and Edison was searching the strange flora of south Florida for new types of bamboo and palm trees.

Many have asked why Thomas Alva Edison, the world's most famous inventor and a very wealthy man, chose this obscure outpost on the west coast of Florida for his winter home. Why did he not choose one of the many fashionable new resorts on the east coast? Why, indeed, did he decide to make a winter home in Florida in 1885?

When Edison arrived in Fort Myers, it was in the outback of Florida, a "cow town" or "Rip Van Winkle settlement" difficult to reach and lacking the sandy shores that most winter residents sought. Early on, towns on the east coast were easily accessible by the Flagler railroad system. Even Key West, the southernmost outpost of Florida, was served by regular and fast steamboats before it was connected to the mainland by railroad in 1912. Henry Plant, the railroad mogul of the west coast, did not think it worthwhile to extend his lines too far south, and the nearest rail connection with the Southern Florida Line was at Punta Gorda, established in 1887 at the north end of Charlotte Harbor. From here the only reliable link to Fort Myers was by steamboat along the Caloosahatchee River with a stopover at Pine Island. It was not until 1904 that Fort Myers could be reached by rail through the Atlantic Coast Line of the former Plant System.

Mina Edison described the perils of early travel to Fort Myers: "It is hard to realize that the approach to Fort Myers was made by water from Punta Gorda, after a ten hours sail, on a boat somewhat fashioned after the type of a New York ferry, or by a haphazard drive of practically twenty-four hours from Arcadia through wild country and with snakes in abundance, swamps and adventure of various description, arriving exhausted but tremendously impressed with the possibilities of a great state."

Edison's choice of Fort Myers in 1885 might have simply been a youthful quest for adventure, but later, as his family and wealth grew, he could easily have moved to the "Gold Coast" of Florida, such as Palm Beach or Miami, the center of social life and luxury in the state. In Miami's Coconut Grove suburb, another famous wizard, inventor of the telephone Alexander Graham Bell, spent his winters.[16] Even Edison's intimate friend Harvey Firestone built a Georgian colonial mansion in Miami Beach, and there the Edisons could have enjoyed the company of the rich and famous during the winter months. But it was typical of Edison to choose to stay in a place like Fort Myers. At heart he was still the country boy longing for a frontier garden in the wilderness. He went his own way, he loved challenge, and he did not follow the crowd. He had his own ideas and stuck to them.

Edison was attracted to Fort Myers in part for the reason that previously had made him leave busy Newark and move to rural Menlo Park, New Jersey. He wanted to get away from the troublesome curiosity of visitors, and "when the public tracks me out here," he said, "I shall simply have to take to the woods."[17] But unfortunately, outside Menlo Park there were not many trees to hide behind and soon crowds of people were coming hoping to get a glimpse of the Wizard of Electricity. When he bought Seminole Lodge, he thought he was safe in the wilderness of south Florida. A Florida friend of Edison's said: "With little civic progress it is no wonder that Edison saw in this tropical *Shangri La* the location he was seeking for his winter home and laboratory experiments, far from the maddening crowd"—a place of rest and seclusion.[18] Once, when asked, "What do you do for amusement?" he answered: "Oh, nothing much. I like to laugh, and I don't care for dancing, and I don't like a crowd, especially if I can't hide myself in it."[19]

Another reason why Edison chose Fort Myers and remained there no doubt was his Green Laboratory, which he had planned from the beginning and established in 1887, two years after his first visit. He wanted a workplace with a machine shop, dynamo, and steam engine next to his home, and where else would this have been possible? Certainly not in the elegant residential areas of Palm Beach or Miami. He loved having a laboratory next door so that he could tinker with his inventions whenever he liked—just as up north in New Jersey, where he had laboratories and a factory next to the elegant Glenmont estate.

Edison never was a temporary "snowbird" from the North. In the real sense of the word he was a Floridian who spent a great deal of his working vacations there on the banks of the Caloosahatchee River.

Sleeping Princess

The splendid isolation of Fort Myers lasted only until the 1920s, when increasing public attention and easy transportation by road became a problem. In 1919 Mina wrote to her son Charles, "It is a beautiful day here again and I love this spot more than ever, fighting for its preservation and beauty, not alone for the few years left to father and me to enjoy it."[20]

The Edisons felt threatened in their tropical paradise. After completion of the Tamiami Trail, the trickle of people coming south became a flood of tens of thousands. The boom was on. According to the *Suniland* magazine: "Lethargy was forgotten. The sleeping princess [Fort Myers] was awake— and madly in love with the good-looking prince. Prices began that sky-rocketing process so typical of Florida towns." The same issue contained a cartoon with the caption: "Gamblers, note!" It showed pirates climbing up from the sea threatening to take possession of Florida with arms and shovels.[21]

In a single day, August 12, 1925, $2,528,000 worth of real estate was sold.[22]

Edison liked privacy. Although he enjoyed publicity to promote his ideas and inventions, he wanted to be able to escape, to hide. Edison wanted "the oblivion of still life" and to be in control of all aspects of his work. On his first visit he learned that he could have access to the International Ocean Telegraph line that passed through the sleepy town on the way to Punta Rassa. In fact, in the 1880s Fort Myers was one of the few places in Florida that could provide this luxury of modern communication. The telegraph made it possible for Edison to keep in touch with his business up north. And finally, there was a unique attraction: he loved to fish, and Fort Myers offered the opportunity to sit quietly on a pier fishing in the calm waters of the Caloosahatchee.

A man is a method, a progressive arrangement;
A selecting principle,
Gathering his like to him wherever he goes.

RALPH WALDO EMERSON, *Spiritual Laws*

⇀ 5 ↽ Edison's Disciple Henry Ford

It is not surprising that Thomas Edison and Henry Ford became friends and soul mates. They had much in common: both were immensely successful innovators, men of simple rural background, self-educated and plain-spoken. They were skeptical of "egg-heads," college-educated experts, and preferred the hardworking tinkerer and his practical way of solving problems by the hunt-and-try method. From the first time they met, Ford became an ardent and lifelong admirer of the inventor. Everything his master said he took as gospel, and Ford lived in Edison's shadow. Edison was, in a way, the encouraging father figure Ford's own father had failed to be.

A Bang on the Table

Their relationship began on August 11, 1886, when Ford, who had been working in the Detroit Edison Company as a mechanic and supervisor, was invited to participate in the annual convention of the Association of Edison Illuminating Companies in New York. The climax of the convention was a banquet at Long Island's Oriental Hotel. After Edison in his speech mentioned the importance of electromotive power, Alexander Dow, the president of the Detroit Edison Company, pointed across the table to Ford and said, "There's a young fellow who has made a gas car." At once Edison was interested and asked questions about the construction. Ford gave details of the engine, the number of cylinders, and the ignition. He even drew a sketch, and when he had finished Edison brought his fist down on the table with a bang and said: "Young man that's the thing—you have it, keep at it. Electric cars must keep near to power stations. The storage battery is too heavy. Steam cars won't do either, for they have to have a boiler and fire. Your car is self-contained—carries its own power plant—no fire, no boiler, no smoke and no steam. Gasoline! You have the thing. — Keep at it." Ford later said, "That bang on the table was worth worlds to me. No man up to then had given me any encouragement but here all at once and out of the clear sky the greatest inventive genius in the world had given me a complete approval."[1]

Competitors

Electromotive power had been one of Edison's many projects, and in 1880 he constructed the first electric railway at Menlo Park, but without commercial success. He had hoped that "in the near future we shall see it supplanting horseflesh and steam; see it drawing carriages over mountains and rivers, without clatter of hoofs or the noise of snorting engines."[2]

It may seem surprising that Edison immediately endorsed Ford's idea of a self-propelled vehicle using a gasoline motor, but he detested waste-producing horses that polluted the city streets and attracted swarms of flies and thought Ford's car might be an alternative. He wanted to put the horse out of business and rightly predicted that the urban horse would become "a luxury, a toy and a pet."[3] We also have to remember that Edison's serious endeavors at constructing an electric automobile came later.

After 1900 he wholeheartedly started research and production of a new source of energy: the alkaline storage battery, which occupied him for a considerable time. He foresaw a great future for it as a source of lighting for isolated houses and for propulsion of submarines. Forgotten was his enthusiastic support of young Henry Ford and his gas car. He wanted to develop a dependable device as motive power for streetcars, trucks, and automobiles. (In 1896 there had been only four automobiles in the United States that would run, but two years later there were eight hundred.)

At this time the Studebaker Company of South Bend, Indiana, "the largest vehicle house in the world" as producer of carriages and wagons, was on the way to becoming an active player in the rapidly expanding automobile industry. In 1902 Edison started to collaborate with Studebaker to develop the first electric vehicle, which he believed would be the final solution in creating self-propelled cars. In 1904 in the *New York Times* he proudly predicted: "Next year I will wager I can take a car of my own design fitted with my motor and battery, and go to Chicago and return in less time, and with more pleasure, than any other machine in existence. There will be no breakdown, no explosion of gas or gasoline, and the trip will be made at an even twenty-five miles an hour."[4]

In his publicity campaign for the Edison battery he envisioned that in the future a large number of gasoline-powered motor cars would pollute congested cities, just as did an early pioneer, the electrical engineer Pedro Salom, who wrote in the *Journal of the Franklin Institute* that electrical motors had no odor whereas "all the gasoline motors which we have seen belch forth from their exhaust pipe a continuous stream of partially unconsumed hydrocarbons in the form of thick smoke with a highly noxious odor. Imagine thousands of such vehicles on the streets, each offering up its column of smell!"[5]

Eventually Edison realized that his electric battery could not compete with internal combustion engines for family cars, and in 1912 he met with Henry Ford again at his West Orange laboratory to talk about the production of a car battery, an electrical starter motor, and a generator that could be used in the Model T. This was the beginning of their lifelong association. Later that year the Edisons drove through Canada to visit the Fords in Dearborn. Thereafter the two families saw each other regularly in New Jersey or Fort Myers.

Edison brought an electric launch, the *Reliance*, to the Caloosahatchee River but never an electric automobile. Why not? Obviously he had the necessary equipment to recharge the batteries of his boat, but he probably did not trust the performance of his own electric automobiles on the cow trails around Fort Myers. Instead, the Edisons used a horse-drawn surrey. But eventually he accepted defeat: in Fort Myers the popular nature trips were not made in electric cars but in Model T Fords, and Edison became a great fan of the "Tin Lizzie" given to him in 1914 by his friend Henry Ford. This was a "wide track" model, offered especially to the "Southern Trade," where this was then the popular wagon track span.[6]

Edison's caretaker, Robert Halgrim, tells of Edison's favorite car, the 1914 Model T Ford:

Mr. Edison would never trade it in for a new one. Mr. Ford had to ride in this old car all the time with his friend and often became rather embarrassed. As time went on Mr. Ford started sending down new parts each year and had the car brought up-to-date each summer when the two men were in the North. Mr. Edison kept the old chassis with wide wheel base because there were only a few paved roads at that time. The present motor is a 1925, having a starter and generator giving electric lights and making it unnecessary to crank the car by hand. The last change was in 1927 when the wheels were put on demountable rims and balloon tires to road test Mr. Edison's goldenrod rubber.

Mr. Ford gave Mr. Edison a Lincoln in 1925 but he never cared for it and gave it to his wife. Mr. Ford asked one day why he insisted on using the Ford in place of the Lincoln. He told him that it was the most convenient car ever made. When pressed for the reason he just chuckled, turned his head and spit some tobacco juice out the side. There were no further questions and they continued to use the old car.[7]

Nature Lovers: Ford and Burroughs

That Ford, one of the prime movers of modern industrialism, the creator of mass-produced motor cars and the assembly line, was a nature lover may seem paradoxical. Ford, however, never forgot his agrarian roots. When he had become rich and influential, he liked to revert back to farm life with its intimate connection to soil, plants, and animals. Since boyhood he had been particularly fond of birds.

Ford became an ardent admirer of the naturalist John Burroughs, who had written many books about country life, nature, and birds. Although not much a reader of books, he immensely valued Burroughs and his tales about nature and bird life. Ford said, "I, too, like birds. I like the outdoors. I like to walk across country and jump fences. We have five hundred bird houses on the farm. We call them our bird hotels, and one of them, the Hotel Pontchartrain—a martin house—has seventy-five apartments."[8]

Ford was saddened by his nature-loving idol's criticism of modern industry and locomotion by motor car. Burroughs said:

Our civilization is the noisiest and most disquieting, and the pressure of the business and industrial spirit the most maddening and killing, that the race has yet experienced. . . . Nature can be seen from lanes and by-paths better even than from the turnpike, where the dust and noise and the fast driving obscure the view or distract attention.

Man demoralizes Nature whenever he touches her.[9]

These comments make a great deal of sense, particularly today.

Despite his attachment to nature, it never occurred to Ford that his cars were jeopardizing the environment. On the contrary, he was of the opinion that putting America on wheels would help ordinary people to enjoy the countryside, plants, and wild animals. Ford complained: "I had never thought of meeting him [Burroughs] until some years ago when he developed a grudge against modern progress. He detested money and especially he detested the power which money gives to vulgar people to despoil the lovely countryside. He grew to dislike the industry out of which money is made. He disliked the noise of factories and railways. He criticized industrial progress, and he declared that the automobile was going to kill the appreciation of nature." Ford wanted to convince America's foremost naturalist of his own beliefs and decided to send the hermit a brand new Model T. "I thought that his emotions had taken him on the wrong track and so I sent him an automobile with the request that he try it out and discover for himself whether it would not help him to know nature better. That automobile — and it took him some time to learn how to manage it himself — completely changed his point of view."[10] The year was 1912, when the sage of the Catskills was seventy years old.

Burroughs initially was perplexed and did not want to accept the present, but later he mellowed under the influence of his eager son Julian, who promised to drive the vehicle. Ford even offered to send someone to teach Burroughs how to run it and promised that there would be no publicity in connection with the gift. When the car arrived in January, Julian immediately began to cruise about the countryside. After some time, his curiosity aroused, the reluctant naturalist decided he also wanted to try his luck, but he had some difficulties. His first mishap came when he ran into a tree. "The little beast sprang for that tree like a squirrel." Later that year he drove into a hay barn and out through the rear wall. He was angry and commented: "I often wish I had never seen a Ford car or any other. All such things create wants which we never knew before. Life is simpler and more satisfying without them." The first meeting between John Burroughs and Henry Ford took place in 1913 in Detroit, and the old man said, "Mr. Ford pleased me and I with him. His interest in birds is keen and his knowledge considerable."[11]

Edison shared Ford's opinion about motor cars, but he was more philosopical:

> Most of us view the automobile principally as a great business and manufacturing achievement. It is—but it is a greater educational achievement. Next to the World War it has done more, perhaps, to jar people out of the ruts of commonplace thinking than almost any other factor in our history. This is not so much because of its stimulus to our transportation as because of its stimulus to our imagination. The wheels of progress—especially those of the automobile—have worked results which might be called miracles. The important mission of the automobile is not the opening of new geography—but the opening up of new opportunity. Their greatest service has been to raise the thinking capacity of society. If there is one evil in the world today for which there is no excuse it is the veil of stupidity.[12]

The Ford Winter Home

In 1913 Edison first met John Burroughs when he and and his family and the Fords visited the sage of the Catskills at his home, Riverby.[13] Edison decided to invite Ford and Burroughs to visit Seminole Lodge the following year.

They both came, Ford with his wife, Clara, and son Edsel and Burroughs alone. Before leaving Detroit, Ford sent an order to the Fort Myers dealer to have three Tin Lizzies ready for him on his arrival: one for Edison, one for Burroughs, and one for himself. Ford and Burroughs arrived on February 23 and were greeted by a crowd of more than a thousand persons. They were escorted to the Edison home by every automobile owner in town—all thirty-one of them. The parade was headed by the three Fords Henry had ordered.[14]

Henry Ford must have enjoyed Fort Myers tremendously. William Bee, sales manager of Edison's battery company, wrote to Edison following the Florida adventure in April 1914: "He says, 'Billy, I had the best time of my life,' and he meant it. Mrs. Ford and Edsel also said they had an excellent time and they were tickled to death."[15]

In 1915 Ford and Edison met again with Burroughs at the Panama-Pacific Exposition in San Francisco when Ford invited Edison and Firestone to Santa Rosa to see the wizard of plants, Luther Burbank, at his farm and then for a motor trip to San Diego. Thereafter they were inseparable friends for the rest of their lives, and the Model T Ford remained Edison's favorite vehicle.

Ford was impressed with the natural beauty of Fort Myers and enjoyed Edison's company so much that he looked for a winter home there. When the property adjoining Edison's went up for sale in 1916, he bought it for $20,000 and they became neighbors. Another property on the other side of Seminole Lodge was for sale, and Mina was hoping that Harvey Firestone would buy it so that "Mr. Edison would feel that he was in seventh heaven."[16] Unfortunately, this did not happen; Firestone preferred Miami.

Ford called his place the Mangoes because of the large number of mango trees on the lot. These mangoes and those on Edison's lot had been brought to Fort Myers by Dr. William Hanson, who came there from Key West in the early 1880s.[17] A fence with a wooden door separated the two properties, but the gate was always open.

Edison was looking forward to his best friend's arrival because he knew that "we will have a fine time playing together." Playing implied many things, among them square dancing on the pier. Ford was keen on this old-fashioned entertainment, and although Edison was not interested, Mina joined in. Before leaving for Fort Myers, Ford had ordered records of "Seaside" and "Heel and Toe Polka" from the Edison studios.

Before the advent of proper roads, camping trips up the winding Caloosahatchee River aboard the stern-wheelers *Suwanee* or *Thomas A. Edison* owned by the Menge brothers were popular distractions. That was before the picturesque river was dredged out to become the straight ditch it is today. These boat trips sometimes went all the way up to Lake Okeechobee or ended at Alva, the little town founded by the legendary Dane Captain Peter Nelson, or at Fort Thompson.

In later years the Fords and Edisons made extensive camping trips to the Everglades. On these trips Edison always was looking for new sources of natural rubber, and he gathered plants, shrubs, and vines which he took back to his laboratory.

Ford, the practical-minded inventor and farm boy, perceived Florida as a possible natural resource for new useful plants. He acquired farmland and the old Hendry house upriver at La Belle, Fort Thompson, where he liked to take long walks, accompanied by his secretary. He also started growing plants for the production of rubber. This venture was in keeping with his idea of combining agriculture with industry.

When not motoring around Fort Myers or making inland trips on the chartered *Suwanee* up the Caloosahatchee to Lake Okeechobee, Edison and Ford took day trips on the ferry to San Carlos Bay and the barrier islands, Sanibel, Captiva, and Pine Island.

Charles, Edison's son by his second wife, Mina, became a good friend of Edsel Ford. According to Charles: "We ventured one morning for a day's outing in a Model T. In those days roads of any description were few and far between in that part of Florida. We steered off the track, the car was over-heated, ran out of water and refused to budge. We waited for the motor to cool and then poured the content of a coffee jug into the thirsty radiator. That got Tin Lizzie moving again, but only temporarily. We got stuck again. Then we did what seemed to be obvious, Edsel and I urinated in the radia-tor—and that proved just enough to get us back to a road where a friendly farmer gave us some water."[18]

The two families regularly wintered in Fort Myers until Edison's death in 1931. The Fords always came down to Florida in a yacht or on their private railroad car, the *Fairlane.* In 1927 Mina Edison complained that the Fords had not come: "I am afraid that you have deserted us for Georgia as I under-stand you have a large tract of land there." As a peace offering, Henry Ford send a new limosine. Mina commented: "It is a stunning Lincoln. It runs beautifully and no noise. The only thing I can see about these things is that they make us lazy. By the movement of my hand I turn on or off the light—windows closes by another movement of the hand and so on. Wonderful luxury these days are gaining on us but I am often questioning in my mind, are they good for us?"[19] This opinion probably also reflected her husband's.

He was always playing practical jokes on everyone in the lab. You could pull one on him if you were good enough. It was his wonderful personality that kept one working for him, to realize that he was working harder than anyone else.

ROBERT C. HALGRIM, FORT MYERS

 **6** **The Green Laboratory**

Why did Edison choose green, the soothing color of nature as the name for what was essentially a big shack, the original Florida electric laboratory, built in 1886–87 and filled with dirty machine tools, steam engine, dynamo, and electric motors? (The laboratory is now on display at Henry Ford's Greenfield Village.) Green was the color of seemingly everything that surrounded Edison in Florida. It probably is a better name for the rubber laboratory later built across McGregor Boulevard where he tested thousands of green plants. That carefully preserved place today also contains dirty test tubes and some crude equipment. But the building is painted green, and now the outside is surrounded by trees and covered with vines.

Machine in the Garden

In March 1885, when Edison purchased land on the Caloosahatchee River for his winter home and big garden, he was determined to add a laboratory and workshop, fully equipped with lathes, tools, steam engine, dynamo, and all other necessities. There would also be electric lighting for the lab and the adjacent houses. He ordered equipment to be shipped south, but in 1886 building the houses had priority and the laboratory was not finished until the following year, when Edison decided he had to come to Fort Myers because his respiratory problems (this time pleurisy) had resurfaced. Fortunately, he soon recovered and could devote himself to completing the laboratory so he would be ready to start working on some of his projects.

The original lab had a water tank on its roof and a fat smokestack that could be seen from the river and became a landmark for navigation. The laboratory was composed of three parts: the boiler room at the far end; the laboratory itself, which occupied one side of the main room and had machinery and dynamos for generating electricity on the other side; and the front part with a little library and office. Completion of the Fort Myers laboratory coincided with another big project: the move of his workplace from Menlo Park to West Orange, New Jersey. He spent most of his waking hours in his laboratories and had a cot installed so he could snatch a few winks of sleep.

From 1887 to 1901 the laboratory was idle, but as soon as the Edisons returned to Florida the steam engine, dynamo, and machine tools began buzzing. In the ensuing years special tools and half-finished prototypes of ongoing projects such as phonographs and storage batteries were shipped to Fort Myers. Edison also brought some of his workforce to Florida, as well as his collaborator, Fred Ott.

The work Edison undertook in his Florida laboratory was a continuation of what he was doing in West Orange. The facilities for development of applied electricity and chemistry were similar to those in the North although on a much smaller scale. The Fort Myers laboratory, however, had certain advantages. In its intimate environment fewer people could interfere and Edison found it easier to concentrate on his work. Another asset was the easy access to the Caloosahatchee River, which enabled him to perform experiments with boats and water sonar equipment. Natural products such as the fibers from different types of bamboo, Spanish moss, palms, the peeling bark of the gumbo limbo tree, insulating material from sponges, and the lustrous surface of seashells were available in abundance. The lush vegetation outside his laboratory invited him to do biological experiments with plants, which he did more of in later years. Edison had a keen mind and was interested in all aspects of nature. He kept bees at Seminole Lodge not only to pollinate the trees and plants but also as a source of wax as raw material. The bees were kept in two old-fashioned conical bee skeps made of coiled bundles of straw. Edison was familiar with this form of beekeeping from his boyhood days in Milan, Ohio.

The 1910 hurricane damaged the pier and the water tank and smokestacks on the roof of the electric laboratory. These were replaced by a smaller chimney and tank on the outside so that it looked as it now does in Greenfield Village. The laboratory that was reconstructed there contains the original equipment, which Edison sold to a local blacksmith but was bought back by Henry Ford in 1928.[1]

The Big Difference

Edison spent long hours in his Florida laboratory, but the atmosphere was totally different from that in the North: the balmy weather, the relaxing mood of the place with its magnificent garden of shady trees and colorful and fragrant flowers, and the enticing possibility of escaping on trips up the river or simply walking out on the pier to fish and meditate. The temptations were great: why not take a break and go on a nature trip in his electric launch or, in later years, the Model T Ford?

Another advantage was the ability to escape the boardrooms of big business, the stream of people, and the nerve-racking pace of the big city. Admittedly there were telegraphs and telephones in Florida, but these links were used sparingly and he was too far away to be summoned to meetings and the formal parties he detested. In West Orange he had staff who shielded him from unnecessary interference and handled day-to-day affairs, but in Florida it was even better. He was mostly out of reach and had the freedom to do what he liked.

The Green Laboratory of Fort Myers never was a center of technological progress like those in Menlo Park or West Orange, but it became a silent spring of inventions, a place where Edison had time to think and plan. And it did become the focus of his last big project: making rubber from goldenrod.

Electric Lights and Other Projects

Although the original phonograph was developed as early as 1877, Edison never lost interest in the project and continually produced new models, aspiring to perfection. Work on the phonograph continued in the electric laboratory at Fort Myers. Some improvements on the incandescent light were also done here, and Jack Beater, a neighbor, received as a gift from Fred Ott an old generator and one of the first lamps with a screw filament: "This is the generator the Old Man used to light the filament in his first carbon lamps. He had it mounted above an old sewing machine treadle, and ran it with a belt. The faster he treadled the brighter the lamp burned, until it burned out. That's the way he found out what voltage the filaments could stand. Then he gave me a lamp bulb. Have to be careful with this. It is one of the first lamps ever made with the screw base. It was made right here in Fort Myers laboratory, from bamboo filament, and you can see where the Old Man, himself, wrote 110 in ink on the neck of the bulb."[2]

A very important development at the turn of the century was creation of a new storage battery. Most of the work required special equipment and chemicals which were available only up north, but some testing was performed in Fort Myers. Nonrechargeable primary batteries as a source of electric current had been around for a long time. Basically such batteries consisted of a container with a solution, usually an acid, into which metallic plates were dipped. Rechargeable "storage" batteries were different: they stored electricity as chemical energy that could be converted into electric current—and, most important, they could be recharged and used over and over again. The original ones were the bulky lead-acid batteries used as stationary power for long-distance telegraphy. Edison, however, wanted to create smaller, more efficient storage batteries to be used as motive power in cars, trucks, and ships. Therefore, he brought some of the prototypes of his new nickel-iron-cadmium batteries south to try them in the hot, humid atmosphere of Florida.

Edison tested new storage batteries in his electric motorboat, the *Reliance*, which he had brought to Fort Myers in January 1904.[3] The boat served the dual purpose of entertainment and experiments. He used it for fishing trips and also for his sonar studies. A generator on shore provided dockside service for recharging the batteries. The boat was kept in a boathouse on the river. Both were destroyed in the hurricane of 1944. The renter of Henry Ford's estate in Fort Myers on wrote on October 22, 1944: "Mrs. Edison's pier is nearly all gone and the RELIENCE [*sic*], Mr. Edison's electric launch that you planned to take to Detroit was washed away and is down the beach about a mile a total wreck. I went down this morning and salvaged the wheel and shaft."[4]

Water Sonar Studies

In 1908 J. B. McClure reported that Edison was working on a sea telephone with which "ships may talk on the ocean."

> Mr. Edison is wide-awake to the possibility of inter-ship communication at sea. His experiments on this device have been confined mainly to the waters of the Caloosahatchee, where he has succeeded in conveying intelligible messages at a distance of one mile. The principle

on which he will endeavor to perfect this instrument is the remarkable facility afforded by water for the transmission of sound. Mr. Edison believes he can even transmit his messages from ship to ship at a distance of at least seven miles. He proposes, after he has perfected his apparatus, to have the large ocean steamers equipped with a steam whistle device, worked by keys somewhat similar to a telegraph instrument, and transmitters after the telephone fashion. Under the waterline of each steamer will be a sounder connected with the captain's cabin by a thin transmitting wire running through a tube. When the captain of one vessel wants to signal another he will sit down at his key-board, turn the steam on his whistle, manipulate the keys, and send his message out into the waves that break against the sound receiver.[5]

These experiments were no doubt performed from the *Reliance* with the help of a local steamer belonging to the Menge brothers. In 1917, during World War I, when Edison became chairman of the Naval Consulting Board, he worked on underwater telephone devices and resonators for the detection of torpedoes and submarines. For this purpose special microphones had to be developed in which the ordinary transducing carbon granules were replaced by minute metal granules. He obtained these granules by using an electrolytic process to plate hogs' bristles with a thin layer of metal. The bristles were then cut into minute pieces and immersed in a bath of caustic potash to dissolve the organic matter, leaving only tiny metal rings. According to Edison, he used "the stuff men dissolved their murdered wives in."[6]

Ford's Historical Project

In a newspaper interview in 1919 Henry Ford proclaimed, "History is more or less bunk." At the time he was rebuked in court and the press for such a statement. He wanted to take revenge in his own way and decided: "I'm going to start up a museum and give people a *true* picture of the development of our country. That's the only history that is worth preserving. We're going to build a museum that's going to show industrial history, and it won't be bunk."[7] To Ford, history was not just the story of political events and battles but should tell of rural America and the march of technological progress, glorifying the triumph of the modern machine.[8]

Ford's sense of history was personal and nostalgic. In the 1920s he planned the first theme park featuring pioneer America in Dearborn, Michigan. He was enthusiastic about the idea of a living historical site at Greenfield Village with authentic old buildings and a museum to preserve the technical development of America. For this project a large number of ancient objects had to be collected because he hoped to recreate the environment in which such pioneers as Edison and Burbank had worked.

Ford greatly admired Edison, and when he decided to memorialize his achievements, he did not stop with acquiring the Detroit power plant of the Edison Illuminating Company. To the best of his abilities he reproduced the early laboratories at Menlo Park and Fort Myers. Showing the real picture to him meant not only all the original machinery and lab equipment but also some of the soil on which it was built.

Edison did not mind relinquishing what was left of the long-defunct Menlo Park buildings; they had been sold to a chicken farmer. When in 1925 Ford wrote to Edison asking to acquire the early electric laboratory from Fort Myers, he got a positive answer. But Ford wanted more—an old Caloosahatchee steamboat to be placed in an artificial river—and to get it he contacted the Menge brothers of Fort Myers.

On their upriver steamboat trips Edison and Ford had become friends with Fred and Conrad Menge, the owners of the Menge Brothers Steamboat Line. They both liked the simple, practical men who were so familiar with all types of ships and boat engines. When Henry Ford was shopping for memorabilia, he most wished to acquire the big stern-wheeler *Thomas A. Edison*, but that was not possible because it had been destroyed by fire in 1914. With the help of "Connie" Menge, however, he found the remains of the seventy-foot *Suwanee* near Moore Haven, where it had been blown ashore in the hurricane of 1926. Here the old steamer had been stranded, and for a time it had become the playground for children and a shelter for the homeless before it was dismantled. Ford rescued the boiler and engine and brought all the parts and Connie Menge, whom he employed to supervise the restoration job, to Dearborn. The reconstruction was made according to drawings by Captain Menge, who had originally built the hull. He built up a top on it with cabins and salons. But Ford did not like that top so it was ripped off and redesigned with open sightseeing decks. Now the stern-wheeler plies a lagoon dug out from an old dried-up riverbed at Greenfield Village. Here one can take a nostalgic ride on man-made Florida waters to the tune of the "Suwanee River."[9]

In 1929, at the opening of Greenfield Village, Ford proudly showed Edison around the meticulously reproduced scene. "Well," he said finally, "what do you think of it?"

Edison shook his head. "Henry, it's 99.9 percent perfect."

"What! There's something wrong?"

"Yes. We never kept the old place this clean."[10]

In many ways the two men were very much alike: self-taught, down-to-earth, and somewhat eccentric. As if mirroring himself, Edison said: "This fellow Ford is like the postage stamp. He sticks to one thing until he gets there." He continued: "As to Henry Ford, my words are inadequate to express my feelings. I can only say to you that, in the fullest and richest meaning of the term, he is my friend."[11]

Edison Gets a New Laboratory

When Ford asked for the original Fort Myers laboratory building to ship to his new historical museum, Edison agreed because Ford offered in exchange the promise of a new laboratory with more modern equipment for his rubber experiments.

Activities in the old lab had been much less intense in the 1920s than in earlier years, no doubt because of Edison's advancing age but also because the original equipment was outmoded. The transfer to Dearborn was not made until 1928, against the wish of Mina Edison and civic organizations, who wanted to keep the buildings that had been a landmark in Fort Myers for more than forty years. According to Mary Nerney, one spring day in 1928 Mina Edison looked out of the window and saw workers dismantling her hus-band's workshop and laboratory. She said, "Dear me, I do wish he would keep out of our backyard." She was referring to their next-door neighbor Henry Ford.[12]

At the opening of Ford's Greenfield Village Museum in Dearborn, Mina reflected nostalgically: "Feel sad to think that Seminole Lodge was disturbed by taking away the little laboratory . . . it is simply a play thing for Mr. Ford. I do not approve of disturbing historical spots. Let things be put and surround the historical spots with beauty. . . . I feel that, deary, is so much more than electric light."[13]

Everything was removed, not only the building and the original equipment and furniture but also one foot of earth beneath it. Preserved in its original form, Edison's Fort Myers lab still sits on Florida soil but is now one of eighty-five historic structures in Greenfield Village.

The new rubber laboratory, painted green (the Green Laboratory), was being completed on the other side of McGregor Boulevard at a cost of $7,000. On the site of the electric laboratory Mina Edison had a small office building constructed which she gave as a birthday gift to her husband in 1929. He used the building as a private laboratory and office so that he did not have to go across the street. Next to it Charles Edison later created Memory Garden with a lily pond surrounded by many beautiful flowers such as bougainvillas, orchids, yellow allamanda, and star jasmine and a statue of his mother, Mina.

The Garden

The beautiful garden with an assortment of colors and shades surrounding the buildings is an integral part of Seminole Lodge and the Green Laboratory. From the trees cheery bird voices were heard, and here Edison could draw a long breath and escape the bustle of a busy world.

In 1929 the garden expert and friend of the Edisons, Henry Nehrling from nearby Naples, wrote:

> There cannot be any doubt that the tropical plantings of Mr. Thomas A. Edison on the shores of the Caloosahatchee, at Fort Myers, form one of the most distinct and enchanting garden paradises in Florida. We all know Mr. Edison as the great inventor. But he is much more than that, he is interested in all branches of natural history. Though the entire place impresses us as a large forest-like park, there are many fine groups and open vistas, showing us the placid and glittering waters of the great river . An avenue of fine old mango trees lines the inside of the garden along the street. These large mango trees are particularly adapted for air gardens.[14]

Mina Edison was a great gardening enthusiast and particularly fond of air plants such as bromeliads and orchids. Her gardening friends presented her with rare specimens. John Kunkel Small, curator of the herbarium of the New York Botanical Garden, who came down to help select plants useful for Edison's rubber project, stayed as a house guest and brought her the giant orchid *Oncidium luridum*, and Henry Nehrling provided bromeliads, which were fastened with copper wire to the trunks of the mango trees.[15]

During a span of more than fifty years, the Edisons created one of the most attractive tropical botanical gardens in the United States. It contains more than four hundred varieties of exotic plants from all over the world, seventy varieties of palms, and fifty different fruit trees. There also is a large variety of rubber trees such as *Ficus elastica* (the India rubber plant), *Ficus altissima*, the cluster fig, and the magnificent Moreton Bay fig, air plants, orchids, and innumerable flowers. Also very important for Edison were different kinds of graceful bamboo, especially the Japanese *Bambusa gracilis*, similar to the species Edison used for his lamp filaments. Cuttings from these plants were given to A. H. Andrews of the nearby Koreshan Colony and now grow thriftily at Estero. Edison neighbor Dr. Franklin Miles also received an assortment of plants. Large portions of the garden across the street were used to grow rubber plants, including a great variety of goldenrod.

The Starlight Express on the road from Tocoi to St. Augustine, Florida. From Edward King, *The Southern States of
North America* (1875).

Thomas Edison's first encounter with Florida: Green Cove
Springs on the St. Johns River. From Edward King, *The
Southern States of North America* (1875).

Thomas Alva Edison, 1885. Edison National Historic Site.

Mina Miller Edison, 1885.
Edison National Historic Site.

Seminole Lodge, Fort Myers. Edison-Ford Winter Estates.

Edison's original Florida electric laboratory, complete with water tank and smokestack. From Florence Fritz, *Unknown Florida* (1963).

Thomas and Mina Edison with friends Henry and Clara Ford in front of the slightly modified electric laboratory before it was shipped to Dearborn, Michigan. Edison-Ford Winter Estates.

The concrete swimming pool, Fort Myers, Florida. Edison-Ford Winter Estates.

Bamboo at Seminole Lodge, Fort Myers. Edison-Ford Winter Estates.

Naturalist John Burroughs. From Burroughs, *Leaf and Tendril* (1908).

Edison the meditative fisherman on the Caloosahatchee River, ca. 1909. Edison National Historic Site.

Birdhouse on pole in the Caloosahatchee River. Edison-Ford Winter Estates.

Thomas Edison and son Charles after a fishing trip on the Caloosahatchee River, 1902. From John D. Venable, *Out of the Shadow* (1978).

Ladies' bonnet adorned with the now extinct Carolina parakeet, Florida's only native parrot. From *Paterson's Magazine* (1883).

The Carolina parakeet by John James Audubon. The bird was caught unmercifully and slaughtered into extinction. From George Dock Jr., *Audubon's Birds of America* (1987).

Camping trip in West Virginia, 1918. Perched on a waterwheel are, left to right, Thomas Edison, John Burroughs, Henry Ford, and Harvey Firestone. From John Burroughs, *Under the Maples* (1921).

Mina and Charles Edison at Seminole Lodge, ca. 1918. Edison-Ford Winter Estates.

"Aladdin—I wish I had sump'n to wish for," cartoon by
Donald McKee, *Judge* (March 1925).

Thomas Edison and Henry Ford visiting Luther
Burbank at his plantation in Santa Rosa, California,
1915. Luther Burbank Museum, Santa Rosa.

Inside the Fort Myers chemical laboratory with Edison in a meditative pose.
Edison-Ford Winter Estates.

Edison in front of the Green
Laboratory with a specimen of
Solidago edisonia, January 1931.
Henry Ford Museum and
Greenfield Village.

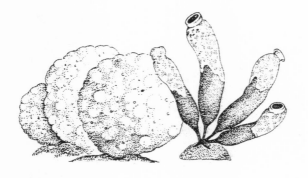

Various types of sponges found in the Gulf of Mexico. From Bob Lollo, *Seashore Identifier* (1992).

The principle of Edison's fluoroscope, 1896. From Glasser, *Wilhelm Conrad Röntgen und die Geschichte der Röntgenstrahlen* (1959).

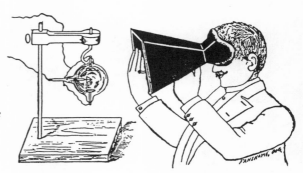

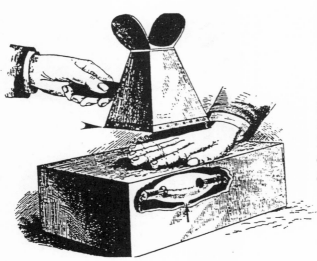

Edison's vitascope, 1896. From R. Brecher and E. Brecher, *The Rays: A History of Radiology in the United States and Canada* (1969).

Edison at Key West working for the Naval Consulting Board, ca. 1917. Florida
Photographic Collection, Florida State Archives, Tallahassee.

The stern-wheeler *Thomas A. Edison* of the Menge Brothers Steamboat Line.
Edison-Ford Winter Estates.

Edison with China's U.S. ambassador, Tien Lai Huang, and Henry Ford in front of the Green Laboratory. From Marian Godown and Alberta Rawschuck, *Yesterday's Fort Myers* (1975).

President-elect Herbert Hoover, with Henry Ford and Harvey Firestone, visiting Edison in Fort Myers, February 11, 1929. From Francis T. Miller, *Thomas A. Edison: Benefactor of Mankind* (1931). Photo by Underwood.

Last birthday in Florida, with Mina, reading congratulations on February 11, 1931. From Francis T. Miller, *Thomas A. Edison: Benefactor of Mankind* (1931). Photo by Acme News.

Sunset on the Gulf of Mexico, 1930. Florida State Hotel Commission, Tallahassee.

Stern-wheeler *Suwanee* plying the waters at Greenfield Village.

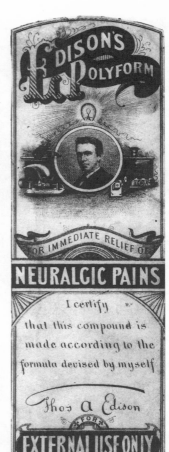

Edison's polyform liniment. Edison National Historic Site.

In quest of American-produced rubber, Harvey Firestone on a visit to Fort Myers on Edison's eighty-first birthday, February 11, 1928. In A. Lief, *The Firestone Story* (1951).

The electric motor launch *Reliance* at the Edison pier. Edison-Ford Winter Estates.

Seminole Indians at La Belle on the Caloosahatchee River. Florida Photographic Collection, Florida State Archives, Tallahassee.

Thomas Edison with his favorite car, the 1914 Ford Model T. Florida Photographic Collection, Florida State Archives, Tallahassee.

Edison, Burroughs, and Ford in Fort Myers. Florida Photographic Collection, Florida State Archives, Tallahassee.

The Edisons with "green" friends, Mr. and Mrs. J. K. Small and C. A. Mosier in Fort Myers. Florida Photographic Collection, Florida State Archives, Tallahassee.

The rubber laboratory (Green Laboratory) in Fort Myers. Photo by the author.

Goldenrod plantation in Fort Myers, Section 5, fertilizer experiments with
Solidago edisonia, February 1934. Henry Ford Museum and Greenfield Village.

Aggressive Florida
land pirates in 1926:
"Gamblers, note."
From *Suniland* 3,
no.4 (1926).

Junior Coronation at the Edison Festival of Light, Fort Myers, 1990. Junior
Queen is T. L. Horton and Junior King is C. G. Sandlin. Official Souvenir
Program, Edison Festival of Light, 1991.

From the guest book of Seminole Lodge, cartoon by "Ding" Jay Darling, winter resident on Sanibel Island. Edison-Ford Winter Estates.

Luther Burbank with spineless cactus at Santa Rosa, California. In *Overland Monthly* (September 1908).

**SEMINOLE LODGE
FORT MYERS, FLORIDA**

There are over one hundred million people in the United States. but only one Ft Myers the flower city of Tropical Florida

Thos A Edison

Edison's view about Florida, Fort Myers, ca. 1925.

*. . . innermost joy in nature and her healing powers
free to all mankind.*

ROBERT UNDERWOOD JOHNSON

 # 7   Camping and Tramping

Over the years there was nothing that the inventor and indoor man enjoyed more than nature trips, by boat or automobile. Was this merely a reflection of a trend of the time or was it typical for the man Edison? The answer is both.

When at the turn of the century in the North, large cities mushroomed and smokestacks of big industry darkened the sky, there was an awakened awareness of the value of American nature. Early nature trips focused on hunting and killing game as a sport, which appealed to men like Teddy Roosevelt with his cowboy machismo. He enjoyed the manly challenge of confronting ferocious animals in the wilderness. But at the same time love of nature for its own sake and preservation of wildlife developed under the influence of two bearded naturalists, John Muir of California and John Burroughs of New York State, the "Two Nature Johnnies."

John Muir once openly criticized President Theodore Roosevelt for his attitude: "Mr. Roosevelt, when are you going to get beyond the boyishness of killing things . . . and are you not getting far enough along to leave that off?"[1]

Call of the Wilderness

The development of North America and exploration of a vast, seemingly hostile wilderness pushing the frontiers of cultivation westward also resulted in ruthless exploitation of natural resources. This devastation was most visually evident along the northern California coastal valleys, where indiscriminate logging destroyed the magnificent redwood forests. Public opinion was finally and slowly aroused, and Congress passed legislation creating national parks. These parks were not only to serve as nature reserves to protect endangered species of animals and plants but also as retreats and recreational resorts for "nerve-shaken" brain workers and businessmen from the industrial centers of the East. At this time the concepts of neuralgia and neurasthenia had been introduced, and Dr. George Beard proposed that "American nervousness is the product of American civilization." This nervous condition was presumed to be the result of steam power, the press, the telegraph, and the sciences and it could be cured by reverting back to nature.[2] By 1903 northerners were seeking a refuge from their tension-producing urban environment, and nature trips became fashionable—fishing and hunting trips or simply camping in the wilderness to listen to birds' songs and enjoy exotic plants and flowers.

Thomas Edison loved camping in the wild as much as he detested formal journeys and dinner parties such as the official receptions and functions he had to attend in New York or Washington or transatlantic trips to London and Paris. Camping was just right for him. He did not have to dress up, could sleep near the roadside, or could stop to investigate rocks and plants. That was probably one reason why in 1885 he embarked on his fateful journey to the west coast of Florida and first encountered Fort Myers. He was restless in the formal atmosphere of his hotel in St. Augustine and wanted to explore the less populated parts of Florida and look for plants that might be useful as filaments in his electric light bulbs.

Flivvers

At the beginning of the century in Fort Myers, nature trips on land had to be made by horse and buggy, but all that changed with the advent of the "horseless carriage." Edison was used to this form of transportation, and he became extremely fond of automobiles and tried to promote the use of electric motors, powered by his own batteries.

In 1904 he bought two steam cars, the "White Steamers," and made his first extensive nature trips to New Hampshire and Massachusetts. The following year he undertook a prospecting excursion to North Carolina. Despite repeated breakdowns, he was quoted as saying in 1906 that "he strongly favors the steam machine for long and rough trips, and declares that it is far superior to the gasoline car for such purposes."[3]

Robert Conot described him as "a confirmed automobile buff who went on outings every Sunday. The greater the speed and the wilder the ride, the better he liked it. He depended on someone else to do the driving—he himself was a helpless driver."[4] When an acquaintance asked his wife, Mina, if her husband drove his own car, she laughed and answered: "He is the most awkward man with his hands I ever saw—he would run a car up a tree or in a ditch, if he tried to drive it."[5]

The first noisy automobile came to Fort Myers in 1908, an Acme, which frightened cattle and people and was described as "emitting clouds of blue smoke as backfiring with explosions."[6] Edison's first automobile in Florida was a "flivver," the Model T presented to him by the motor king himself in 1914, when Henry Ford and his wife made a long visit to Seminole Lodge. John Burroughs was invited to join the party. The call to nature moved Edison and Ford, the greatest proponents of, "if not a fictitious civilization, then a highly mechanized one and its mass culture. There was a touching incongruity, therefore, in their tour to the Everglades and the cypress forests, under the guidance of John Burroughs."[7]

Edison boasted to reporters from the *New York Times*: "We'll go down to the Everglades and revert back to Nature. We will get away from fictitious civilization." But characteristically he added a caveat: "If I get an idea I will leave my companions temporarily and go to my laboratory there to work it out."[8] For Edison, work always had priority even during holidays. In West Orange, Mina had to have a small laboratory installed in their house, Glenmont, to keep her husband at home or he might not come back from work for days on end.

The Grass Lake

With his pals Edison planned a nature trip to the cypress forests and great silent mystery of the Everglades, which the Seminole Indians called Grass Lake. It was their only remaining refuge, where they had privacy and a limited freedom to shape their own lives. The name describes it precisely: it is a vast waterland, a swamp of sawgrass with islands of trees.

John Burroughs commented: "It started as a hot day and most of us dressed very light but before departure Mina Edison told us to wear long-sleeved shirts because of the saw grass, the most abundant vegetation of the Everglades. It gets its name from the serrated edges of its leaves that makes nasty scratches on bare legs and arms of anyone foolish enough not to wear long pants and long-sleeved shirts."[9]

At first, Burroughs did not want to go to Florida. He had been disappointed with his previous travels south. Although on his trip to Jamaica he escaped ice and snow, he later lamented about "a lost February," and he abhorred the tropical scene. He exclaimed that he was tired of everlasting summer, with no spring, no autumn, nothing tender, nothing to love or take to heart. To him the tropics were formal and stiff, and all vegetation was covered with thorns or ticks. He would have preferred to throw himself into the lap of nature without being pricked or bitten. "To our northern eyes, Nature in the tropics has little tenderness or winsomeness. She is barbaric; she is painty and stiff; there is no autumn behind her and no spring before; she has no sentiment; she does not touch the heart." He even went so far as to say, "I cannot conceive of any poetry ever being produced in the tropics." Like his friend John Muir, he felt alienated in the southern environment because he was more used to the mountains and the woods of the North.[10]

At first the barbaric splendor of Florida both fascinated and repelled Burroughs. But in the company of friends, he soon felt more at ease and ultimately he was happy to have made the trip:

> February 25. Here at Ft Myers, Florida, with the Edisons and Fords.... Midsummer weather. A real tropical scene, reminds me of Jamaica and Honolulu. I can eat these oranges and grape-fruit. A coconut tree loaded with fruit out of my window. Pretty nearly an earthly paradise here, lacks only the mountains to lift up toward heaven. Healthy, good, mind active.—We fish and sail and walk and motor and loaf on the broad verandas. Yesterday we returned from a two day's trip to a cypress forest 60 miles in the interior. We slept in tents and dined and supped on wild turkey and venison. We had two guides and a cook. Mr. Edison and Mr. Ford are as young as I am, but not younger. Mrs. Ford had a horror of snakes before her all the time, but is glad she went. We only saw garter snakes.[11]

The group enjoyed their trips into the Everglades and were enthusiastic about all the strange birds they saw. At that time the Big Cypress Swamps resounded with the clacking sounds of the bills of black-and-white-plumed wood storks. These birds wading along the mud flats looked like old men with their black, wrinkled, bald heads. Burroughs had never seen anything like them; they could have been prehistoric creatures. He was also impressed by the the white ibis: "In Florida, in the spring when the mating instinct is strong, I have seen a flock of white ibises waltzing about the sky, going through various intricate movements, with the precision of dancers in a ballroom quadrille." Burroughs, America's best-known writer about birds, gave a superb description of the brown pelican:

There are the clumsy-looking but powerful winged birds, the brown pelicans, usually in a line of five or six, skimming low over the waves.— Often gliding on set wings for a long distance, rising and falling to clear the water—coasting, as it were, on a horizontal surface, and only at intervals beating the air for more power. They are heavy, awkward-looking birds with wings and forms that suggest none of the grace and beauty of the usual shore birds. They do not seem to be formed to cleave the air, or to part the water, but they do both very successfully. When the pelican dives for his prey, he is for the moment transformed into a thunderbolt. He comes down like an arrow of Jove, and smites and parts the water in superb style. When he recovers himself, he is the same stolid, awkward-looking creature as before.[12]

Edison, who loved jokes, preferred another popular description: "A gorgeous bird is the pelican, whose bill can hold more than his bellican, he can put in his beak, food enough for a week, but I'm blest if I can see how in hellican."[13]

Burroughs, a more serious man, also had his opinions about the soaring flight of the tropical frigate bird that rides the airy billows in great circles and spirals over the coastal waters. He thought it was peculiar that the grace of motion was given to such an unclean bird, a repulsive scavenger that is called man-of-war because of its habit of robbing fish that other birds have caught.

Strange Fascination

Burroughs, who always looked for natural explanations of the wonders of "creation," was happy in the company of Edison, who offered physical and chemical solutions to mysteries of life. Despite his reservations about the South, Burroughs was very pleased with his trip to Florida and enjoyed the relaxing atmosphere in Fort Myers with Edison and Ford, whom he found to be "good play-fellows." They must have made a happy trio, Burroughs the sage Yankee naturalist, Edison with his never-ending curiosity, wisdom, jokes, and good stories, and Ford with his knowledge of machinery and his love of birds.

In the evening, when they returned exhausted from their trips, John Burroughs, his long, white beard making him look like Santa Claus, quoted Walt Whitman, his mentor: "O strange fascination of these half-known half-impassible swamps, infested by reptiles" and "Again in Florida I float on transparent lakes, I float on the Okeechobee, I cross the hummock-land or through pleasant openings or dense forests." These camping trips to the Everglades were so pleasant that Burroughs invited Edison and Ford to come the next year on a camping trip to the Hudson River and his native Catskill Mountains. "There you will see my mountains, a land of brooks of water, of fountains and depths that spring out of valleys and hills. There we can do some nice trout fishing in the best water of the world, we can watch birds and porcupines."[14]

Turning Vagabond

The much publicized camping trips with Ford, Firestone, and Burroughs in New England and the Great Smoky Mountains from 1916 to 1924 were Edison's idea and an extension of their excursions along wild Florida trails into the Everglades and the Big Cypress Swamp.

In 1916 John Burroughs reluctantly agreed to join a motor trip through the Adirondacks with Edison and Firestone. Henry Ford could not come because he was tied up at work and busy with his efforts to promote peace. It was the year of the first Zeppelin raid on Paris and the battle of Verdun. Public opinion on the war was divided, but President Woodrow Wilson and Henry Ford made attempts to broker peace.

These wealthy industrialists referred to their trips as excursions into "Nature's Laboratory." John Burroughs, the writer-philosopher and chronicler of the expeditions, summed it up when he wrote that all the unpleasant features were strained out or transformed and in retrospect all was enjoyable, even the discomforts:

> It often seemed to me that we were a luxuriously equipped expedition going forth to seek discomfort, —dust, rough roads. Heat, cold, irregular hours, accidents — is pretty sure to come to those who go a-gypsying in the South. But discomfort, after all, is what the camper-out is unconsciously seeking. We grow weary of our luxuries and conveniences. We react against our complex civilization, and long to get back for a time to first principles. We cheerfully endure wet, cold, smoke, mosquitoes, black flies, and sleepness nights, just to touch naked reality once more.[15]

The annual two-week auto trip in 1918 was bigger than ever. This time, in addition to Ford, Firestone, and Burroughs, Edison had invited Edward Hurley, a high official in the Wilson administration. Their destination was the Great Smoky Mountains. But this camping trip was overshadowed by clouds of war. The trip took place in August 1918 during the last months of World War I, and the campers saw eastbound army trucks loaded with soldiers. They met weary families whose boys had fought in France. The talk around the campfire dwelled on the fatuous Kaiser and the operations of the U.S. Navy. Edison and Burroughs, although enjoying living in the wild, felt cut off from world news and eagerly looked for newspapers when they came to towns.

Edison would sit in front, next to the driver, the only seat in the automobile he liked; the others rode behind. They passed through the mountain resorts of Warm Springs, Hot Springs, and Sweet Water Springs. In West Virginia old-fashioned gristmills driven by overshot waterwheels, some still in use, were seen along the way. At Horseshoe Run Creek the party stopped and the men perched on the waterwheel of a mill and had their picture taken. While hiking Burroughs closely observed his friends Ford and Edison:

> Partly owing to his more advanced age, but mainly, no doubt, to his meditative and introspective cast of mind, Mr. Edison is far less active than is Mr. Ford. When we would pause for the midday lunch, or to make camp at the end of the day, Mr. Edison would sit in his car and read, or curl up, boy fashion, under a tree and take a nap, while Mr. Ford would inspect the stream or busy himself in getting wood for the fire. Mr. Ford is a runner and a high kicker, and frequently challenged some of the party to race with him. . . . He has expressed himself through his car and his tractor engine. They typify him; not imposing, nor complex, less expressive of power and mass than of simplicity, adaptability, and universal service, they typify the combination of powers and qualities which make him a beneficent, a likable, and unique personality. Those who meet him are invariably drawn to him.[16]

Burroughs would have liked to be the center of attention, but that was not the case. One can sense a slight feeling of envy toward Edison, the man with an unfailing memory and logical thinking who appeared to be a bit crude: "Essentially the same thing may be said of Mr. Edison: his first and leading thought has been, what can we do to make life easier and more enjoyable to my fellow-men? He is a great chemist, a trenchant and original thinker on all the great questions of life, though he has delved but little into the world of art and literature—a practical scientist, plus a meditative philosopher of profound insight."[17]

But Burroughs also expressed admiration: "His humor is delicious. We delighted in his wise and witty sayings. A good camper-out, he turns vagabond very easily, can go with his hair disheveled and clothes unbrushed as long as the best of us, and can rough it week in and week out and wear his benevolent smile. He eats so little that I think he was not tempted by the chickenroosts or turkey-flocks along the way, nor by the cornfields and apple-orchards, as some of us were, but he is second to none in his love for the open and wild nature."[18]

Burroughs commented: "Camp-life is a primitive affair, no matter how many conveniences you have, and things of the mind keep pretty well in the background. Occasionally around the campfire we drew Edison out on chemical problems, and heard formula after formula come from his lips as if he were reading them from a book. As a practical chemist he perhaps has few, if any, equals in the country. It was easy to draw out Mr. Ford on mechanical problems. There is always the pleasure and profit in hearing a master discuss his own art."[19]

In 1921, after Burroughs's death, the party was joined by President Warren Harding and in 1924 by President Calvin Coolidge. The simple camping trips finally degenerated into "a kind of travelling circus" attended by reporters from press and film.[20]

Come forth into the light of things,
Let nature be your teacher.

WILLIAM WORDSWORTH

 # 8   Edison, Nature Lover

In 1924 a friend who just had met Edison after his return from Fort Myers reported: "His face was ruddy, his grey-blue eyes were sparkling, and his smile was infectious as he spoke of his various excursions out along the river banks. His refusal to grow old, coupled with a keen response to Nature's moods, explains much of his marvellous vitality."[1]

Edison realized that nature in Florida had relaxing and healing properties. His love of nature was often pragmatic and an expression of curiosity, although it was said that he had "a deep and genuine sensibility for the beauty of the natural world when he had time for it."[2]

Eye-Openers

During the early hectic years in the Newark workshop Edison's mind and activities were totally occupied with experiments and development of his inventions. During this period he married his first wife, the teenager Mary Stilwell, whose activities were limited to her house and children. There was no time for gardening and nature trips even after the family moved to rural

Menlo Park, New Jersey. Edison's only diversion was fishing trips with his co-workers. In his own words: "I had been to Quogue, Long Island, to get away from the laboratory and think. And when pressure became too great at Menlo Park, we used to go down and hire a sloop and go fishing off Sandy Hook." On one of these trips Edison purportedly fished for two days and nights without a bite and the "boys" had to hoist the anchor to make him quit.[3]

In the beginning Edison felt most at home in the stuffy atmosphere of his laboratory. But despite his total devotion to electricity, smelly chemical experiments, and mechanical gadgets, over the years he developed a keen interest in nature, particularly in Florida, although he did not adopt the romantic inclination and poetical language of the often-quoted lovers of Florida Ralph Waldo Emerson and William Bartram ("How happily situated is this retired spot of earth. . . .").

After Edison married his second wife, Mina Miller, the garden of their new home, Glenmont, in Llewellyn Park, became an important part of their estate in New Jersey, with fruit trees, lawns, and exotic shrubs from around the world. Tropical plants, flowers, and palms for display were grown here in a greenhouse and potting shed. Even though he enjoyed his gardens in New Jersey and Florida, Edison also took an inquisitive view of plants and soil, and one of his prime interests in nature was as a source of new raw materials for constructions and inventions.

Only later in life, much through the influence of Mina, did he become interested in exotic plants and flowers for their own sake. Others who inspired Edison's interest in nature were the naturalist John Burroughs, Henry Ford, and the gardener Luther Burbank. The seeds of the friendship with Burroughs were sown when Mina talked admiringly about his bird books. At the time, he was the greatest writer of nature essays in America. Bird-watching had become fashionable at the turn of the century and was promoted by Teddy Roosevelt, who loved hunting and hiking with the bearded naturalist. These trips were much publicized and contributed to Roosevelt's popularity.

Henry Ford also opened up Edison's eyes to things outside his workshop and laboratories. Throughout his life Ford always remained attached to outdoor life, and he introduced Edison to the naturalist.

Edison's interest in nature undoubtedly arose in Florida, where he made nature trips up the Caloosahatchee and into the hammock lands of the Everglades. It was in Fort Myers that the friendship of Edison, Ford, Burroughs,

and later Harvey Firestone was the spark for his extensive nature trips into the Great Smoky Mountains and New England. Edison once revealed:
"While mankind appears to have been gradually drifting into an artificial
life of merciless commercialism, there are still a few who have not been
caught in the meshes of this frenzy and who are still human and enjoy the
wonderful panorama of the mountains, the valleys and the plain."[4]

Cherchez la femme!

How did Mina induce Edison's interest in "green activities"? Wasn't she the
instigator of the changes that took place after the death of Mary, the move to
Florida, and Edison's interest in plants and wildlife? The answer is a qualified yes. Mina certainly inspired a new view on life and created aspirations
that never before had crossed his mind. She was influential in promoting a
curiosity for nature, especially birds. She said of her husband: "He loves his
garden, and motoring is his favorite recreation."[5]

Her own interest in nature dated from when as a young girl she spent
summers at Chautauqua Lake in southwestern New York State. The Chautauqua Assembly set a standard for education in America in an era when
school was not mandatory. This Methodist training center, cofounded by
her father, Lewis Miller, not only gave instruction in religious and cultural
matters but also offered nature walks and a very active Bird and Tree Club.
Mina clearly contributed to Edison's interest in nature during their courtship in the summer of 1885, when they visited the Lewis Miller cottage at
Chautauqua Lake.

Mina's influence is more apparent in Edison's later years, both at Glenmont and in the big garden at Seminole Lodge in Fort Myers. Mina loved
birds and watched with interest the great variety of her feathered friends in
Florida, and she tried to protect them from predators and human hunters.
Both up north and in Fort Myers she set up many birdhouses and birdbaths
and chased away cats and squirrels that threatened her favorite companions.
At Seminole Lodge she even erected birdhouses on poles in the waters of
the Caloosahatchee River out of reach of predators.

Shameful Slaughter

The popularity of egret feathers in fashions of the late nineteenth century
led to national interest in protecting wild animals. It is the story of woman's
vanity and man's greed. Gathering and selling wild bird plumes in Florida
had become a very lucrative business. In 1887 nearly 40 percent of all prod-

ucts exported from Fort Myers were bird plumes, alligator, panther, and bear skins, and stuffed animals. Seeing this dirty trade firsthand touched the hearts of the Edisons.[6]

In New York, Paris, and London the fancy feathers were in such high demand by the millinery trade that they were literally worth their weight in gold. Practically all hats and bonnets displayed in ladies' magazines of the 1880s (such as *Paterson's* of Philadelphia) were adorned with plumes. In 1892 a single agent reported that he had shipped 130,000 birds from Florida for millinery purposes, and in 1910 the plumage business in New York was valued at about $17 million.

Most sought after were the dainty feathers of the snowy egret, which carried a beautiful spray of fifty plumes on its back during the breeding season (the aigrettes). Egrets' and herons' plumage is most elaborate during nesting time. As John J. Audubon describes it:

Delicate in form, beautiful in plumage,
and graceful in its movements. . . . .
Watch its motions, as it leisurely walks
over the pure sand beaches of the coast of Florida,
arrayed in the full beauty of its spring plumage.[7]

Hunters would shoot the poor creatures to take their feathers, leaving young birds as unprotected prey for predators and unhatched eggs in the nests. A pioneer conservationist wrote: "I saw so many things I don't like to even think about it any more, as it gets close to your heart when you see literally thousands of starving and dying birds being devoured by vultures and crows."[8]

Other birds hunted for their feathers were the roseate spoonbill, called by some "pink chicken" (because they were also good to eat), the reddish egret, and the white ibis. The ruthless slaughter of birds for plumes soon put some species in danger of extinction. The reddish egret was wiped out of Florida before the feather trade was outlawed. Only isolated rookeries survived in remote areas of the Caribbean. It has only recently made a timid comeback on Honeymoon Island near St. Petersburg. Three of the birds have been seen there, and they are a bird-watcher's delight.[9] The Carolina parakeet, Florida's only native parrot, beautifully painted by Audubon, was hunted for its wing feathers and head, which were used to adorn hats and bonnets. Many thousands were killed for the millinery trade or trapped and sent north as cage birds. The gay parakeets lived in all sections of Florida, in hammocks or swamps. This bird was was not only strikingly colored but also sociable, making it a good pet. It came to the gardens of the early settlers, where it enjoyed eating mulberries and was seldom seen alone. Its devotion to wounded companions enabled hunters to annihilate large numbers, for not a member of a large flock would leave an injured bird alone.[10] According to George Dock, the last of these magnificent native North American birds was seen in 1920 in an almost inaccessible swamp in the Everglades.[11] But as late as 1925, a Fort Myers old-timer, Julia Hanson, said: "Carolina paroquets, roseate spoonbills and egrets were here in thousands; but the 'sportsmen' and plume hunters have virtually exterminated them."[12]

Plume hunting was cruel and destructive. Charlton Tebeau explains: "In 1901 the Florida legislature passed the first law to stop the killing of wild birds for plumage. But enforcement was another matter. It would be difficult at best, and no money was appropriated for carrying out the law."[13]

Finally, the National Audubon Society of Florida hired men to protect some of the endangered rookeries, but in 1905, while on duty, the warden Guy Bradley was murdered by a poacher at Cape Sable. The killer was arrested in Key West but freed by the court when nobody would witness against him. Columbus McLeod was the second victim, gunned down by poachers at Charlotte Harbor in 1908.[14] These men did not die in vain, for their murders created outrage and inspired the 1910 Audubon Plumage Act of the New York State legislature, which prohibited trade in plumes. But in Florida the slaughter continued, and the feathers were sold to European millineries that made plumed hats and could legally export them to the United States.

The barbaric trade ended only when fashions changed. In a letter salvaged from the *Titanic* in 1912, a milliner and boa manufacturer expressed his concern that "the tendency for shaped hats" in the new season would damage the feather business.[15]

The Wizard of Plants

In 1915 Ford, Edison, and the tire king Harvey Firestone met at the great Panama-Pacific Exposition in San Francisco to celebrate Edison Day, marking the thirty-sixth anniversary of the electric light. It featured the "Electric Dinner," at which an all-electric kitchen was demonstrated. While in San Francisco the three industrialists went to visit Luther Burbank at his farm in Santa Rosa. The editor of the *San Francisco Examiner* wrote that "nothing could be more fitting than that the Wizard of the West should extend welcome and greeting to the Wizard of the East on his visit to California." Another San Francisco newspaper hailed Burbank as "the Edison of horticultural mysteries."

Burbank, the "wizard of plants," bridged the gap between inanimate objects such as phonographs and automobiles and living nature. He raised thousands of seedlings to obtain a single improved variety. He was the Henry Ford of the art of hybridization by mass production and the epitome of modern technology in plants and flowers. Progress was everywhere, and there seemed to be no limit to what could be achieved, not only in the laboratories inventing new technology but also in the realm of plants. This optimism fitted well into the Lamarckian concept of nature that "nothing but acquired characters may be inherited."[16] Heredity was seen as nothing but stored environment which could be manipulated. Burbank was considered a miracle man, and people joked that "he can cross the milkweed with the eggplant, to produce an omelette."[17]

Burbank had achieved miracles with plants just as Edison had with electricity. So when in San Francisco, Edison was curious to meet the man with whom he had corresponded. Edison said to his friends: "Let's go and see this remarkable man Burbank while here. He is constantly busy creating new flowers and plants. Not like the old botanists who collected dried, shriveled plant mummies with no soul. No, this fellow knows that plants are not stagnant but can be changed to come up with new varieties of flowers with beautiful colors and forms. Did you know that by cross-breeding he even managed to grow a spineless cactus, good as cattle feed?" The visit to Santa Rosa established a firm bond among the three men, and they were to meet again in Florida.

Nature Friends

Testimony to Edison's interest in nature comes from many sources, including his neighbors in Florida, Franklin Miles and Henry Nehrling. In the winter of 1904–5 Dr. Franklin Miles, founder of the Miles Pharmaceutical Company of Alka Seltzer fame, left his flourishing business in Elkhart, Indiana, and visited Fort Myers for health reasons. He liked it so much that he returned the following year to settle permanently and started a second career growing plants. He established plantations on both sides of the Caloosahatchee River, cultivating eggplants, green peppers, cucumbers, beans, tomatoes, squash, sugarcane, gladioluses, bananas, and citrus. His plantation included sugar mills and sawmills, a packing house for tomatoes, and a stone crusher to smash oyster shells into fertilizer.

He became a good friend of the Edisons, and they often spent Sundays together either in Fort Myers or at Miles's vacation home on Captiva Island. Their common interest was plants, particularly newly imported ones, and they exchanged cuttings and seeds. Miles's daughter Louise acknowledged: "We knew the Edisons quite well because Daddy and Mr. Edison were persons who had inquiring minds. They wanted to know what made things run. When Mr. Edison was experimenting with trying to find filaments for the light bulb, he imported a lot of bamboo plants. He gave Daddy roots and cuttings. The bamboos that grow on the river, Mr. Edison gave us. And then he became interested in rubber, he gave Daddy quite a lot of cuttings from his rubber trees."[18]

The garden enthusiast and botanist Henry Nehrling of nearby Naples was another good friend of the Edisons. Nehrling had come to Florida from Milwaukee and planted a marvelous garden with many exotic specimens at Gotha, Orange County. But in 1917, when a hard frost hit Florida, many of his most valuable plants were destroyed, so at the age of sixty-three he decided to start a new garden at Naples, sixty miles south of Fort Myers.

Nehrling remembered about Edison:

Recently (April 27th, 1927) he and Mrs. Edison spent almost an entire day with me in my garden here at Naples, where I have accumulated about 100 species of Ficus. Though having celebrated on February 11th, his eightieth birthday, he showed himself as alert and enthusiastic, as interested and desirous of knowledge as any young student. In fact, I have never met with anyone who was so elated and delighted about all the species I cultivate, the correct botanical name, their age, where they came from and the quantity and quality of their milky sap. With the exception of *Ficus elastica*, he found only one other species that met his approval as a rubber yielding plant—*Ficus utilis* of Southeast Africa.

After we had looked over all the plants in the grounds we retired to my little house, where both Mr. and Mrs. Edison looked over with profound interest my books, my manuscripts and my photographs of Ficus species. In every respect this famous inventor, one of the greatest of all times, showed himself as a model of modesty, as a thorough scientist and as a most systematic worker—a most wonderful man. It is only necessary to come in contact with him to feel the power of his eminence and greatness and charm of his personality.[19]

Other nature-loving friends and plantsmen called at Seminole Lodge. The famous botanist John Kunkel Small, head curator of the herbarium of the New York Botanical Garden, was one of them. He likely had a great influence on Edison's attitude toward matters of preservation. Edison collaborated with him on the identification of rubber plants, and both men were concerned about the wanton destruction caused by drainage and fire in south Florida. To make his case, Small had written *From Eden to Sahara: Florida's Tragedy*, illustrated with photographs of hammocks and pine forests before and after their destruction by humans.[20]

Another New Yorker who visited the Edisons was Charles William Beebe, the pioneer of deep-sea exploration with the bathysphere. His discussions with the Edisons, however, were not about the secrets of the sea but concerned birds. Beebe, originally an ornithologist, started the live bird collection at the New York Zoological Park.

Edison's Florida "green friends" were the naturalist Charles Torrey Simpson of Little River, David Fairchild of Coconut Grove, and Charles Mosier from Viscaya, Miami. Mosier, Small, and Fairchild explored the hammock region, which was to become the Royal Palm State Park. Simpson was fascinated by the unique and colorful Florida land snails and had a collection of twenty thousand species of shells. All three men were ardent supporters of the idea of creating a national park in Florida.

Shut Up and Fish!

When doing my research on Edison in Fort Myers, one morning at breakfast I sat next to an old man who sported a cap with the inscription: "Shut up and fish." If there had been such a headdress in Edison's time, I am sure he would have worn it. Fishing was his favorite pastime occupation, sport, and source of inspiration.

After Edison came to Florida, he became interested in fish and other forms of aquatic life. Edison was not a very successful fisherman in terms of big catches, but the sessions on the pier were a welcome opportunity to get away from the house and laboratory and to enjoy peace and relaxation in his own fashion: meditating on new inventions. He agreed with his friend Herbert Hoover, who claimed that there were but two occasions when Americans respected privacy—when one was praying or fishing. While in Florida Hoover said: "Fishing is the chance to wash one's soul with pure air . . . it brings a quieting of hate, a rejoicing that you do not have to decide a darned thing until next week."[21]

Even though both liked fishing, one was a fly-fishing elitist and the other simply a contemplative angler. But the notion of the purely meditative angler is an exaggeration. In 1912 Edison bitterly complained about the scarcity of fish in the Caloosahatchee. Compared to previous years, the number of mullet and other catches was drastically reduced, and he caught only a few catfish. This probably was the result of the increased flow of fresh water from Lake Okeechobee and uncontrolled drainage of sewage from the expanding town into the river. Edison was angry. He blamed increased fishing with seine and gill nets and advocated a ban on net fishing (a prohibition that in Florida came into effect on July 1, 1995).

Mina, as always receptive to his complaints, came up with a brilliant idea: why not pull strings in Washington? She had heard about the U.S. government's efforts to improve fishing by replanting young fish in rivers. On November 15, 1912, she wrote to the Department of Commerce:

> Is it within the jurisdiction of your department to stock a portion of the Caloosahatchee River, which runs from Lake Okeechobee in Florida to the Gulf of Mexico, with young fish (except catfish) which would be apt to live in this river.
>
> I am particularly anxious to have stocked the small creeks or streams which run into the river proper at a distance of eighteen miles from the mouth of the river. Opposite to this particular point is our home where we live the greater part of February and March each year, and Mr. Edison would thoroughly enjoy the good fishing you could probably make possible.
>
> Any efforts you may make to this end would be thoroughly appreciated by myself and Mr. Edison.

The following day the commissioner of fisheries replied: "The Bureau will be very glad to comply with your wishes relative to the matter of stocking with suitable fishes the small streams tributary to the Caloosahatchee River, Florida, in the vicinity of your winter home." She soon received application forms listing species available for implantation. Mina had only to tick the relevant boxes and return the form. Mina's request was probably followed by implantation of little fishes into Twelve Mile River, Billy's Creek, Yellow Fever Creek, and other tributaries of the Caloosahatchee River. One may hope that Edison's fishing luck improved during the following years. But in 1920 Mina wrote to her son Charles again, complaining: "Fishing is no good at all this year, but I am going to have it stocked this summer so I hope another year the fish will be in abundance. The only thing is that everybody wants to come and fish off our pier."[22]

Mina Edison commented: "When we first came to Fort Myers Mr. Edison used to fish from the bulkhead. He takes a great interest in fishing, though he doesn't catch much except catfish. We used to laugh over his excitement when he landed a big catfish. He was delighted when he caught a record tarpon. His greatest joy, however, was to catch a shark, which he would do occasionally. The fish got more and more elusive. And the pier got longer and longer, going out into the river fifty feet at a time. It is now 1,140 feet long, and I don't suppose it's stopped growing yet."

Silver King

In the 1880s catching the jumping silver-sided tarpon become a craze of the rich and famous. Each spring vast schools of these fish move in from the south, leaping and gleaming in the sun, escaping the heat and following crabs and other small prey to the cooler North. Indians used to spear them with harpoons. Sportsmen did not catch tarpon for their flesh but rather as game fish. Karl Bickel, onetime president of United Press and author of *The Mangrove Coast*, relates: "Until 1885, it was gospel along the Florida gulf coast that a tarpon could never be caught with ordinary tackle and bait and that if a tarpon tangled on such gear the tackle would break in less than five minutes."[23]

But that all changed when tarpon fishing with reel and line was successfully attempted with special gear introduced by New York City sportsman W. H. Wood. This gear became a sensation among the gentlemen sportsfishermen and prompted an article in the London *Observer* of August 25, 1886: "Here, at last, there is a rival to the black bass of North America, to the *silurus glanis* of the Danube, to our own European salmon, and possibly even to the sturgeon, were that monster capable of taking a hook and holding it in its leech-like sucker of a mouth. Sportsmen may yet go to Florida for the *tarpon*, as they now go to the Arctic zone for reindeer, walrus, and musk-ox."[24]

The largest beast taken with rod and reel was one recorded at St. James City weighing 184 pounds. The area around Fort Myers and Charlotte Harbor became famous for tarpon fishing. St. James City on Pine Island and Punta Rassa were referred to by some as the headquarters of tarpon enthusiasts. Tarpon House was a small hotel at Punta Rassa run by George Shultz, the telegraph operator of the Havana cable. It was at the Tarpon House on his first visit in 1885 that Thomas Edison decided to move to Fort Myers.

Tarpon scales were admiringly described by a contemporary enthusiast: "The tarpon is one of the most elegantly formed denizens of the ocean, and certainly among the most brilliant in hue, its scales gleaming like brightly-burnished silver in the sunlight. These average about six inches in circumference on an adult male, and are so clear that I have seen advertisements of hotels stamped on them. They were also occasionally used as visiting cards by lovers of novelty."[25]

One of the first famous visitors to Edison at Seminole Lodge was George Granville, third Duke of Sutherland and cousin to Queen Victoria. The bearded duke was an easygoing, eccentric, big man with informal manners who liked to run locomotives and steam engines, and he was a mighty fisherman. When he came to America, it was not only for tarpon fishing but also to be alone in the company of pretty Claire Blair, the widow of a Highland regimental officer who had been killed while hunting in the hills of Scotland.[26]

Edison had met Granville earlier in New York and had shown him the mysteries of electric lighting in the home of one of his clients. He had mentioned his new place in Fort Myers and how good fishing was there. The duke was crazy about tarpon fishing. He had built himself a comfortable house north of St. Petersburg, in Tarpon Springs. In spring, during the fishing season, he made frequent trips down the Gulf Coast and took the opportunity to visit the famous inventor. When a visiting New York reporter told Edison that the duke was on his way from Tampa, Edison said that he was happy to accommodate him "with all the sand spurs that he wanted."[27]

Charles Edison had joyful memories of fishing expeditions on the Caloosahatchee with his father. The most memorable was the time when they went out on the river in the electric launch, the *Reliance*:

We'd go out in a small boat together and troll a great deal. There was a world of fish in those days. Then as now the greatest catch was a tarpon. That was the king of all fish down there. The first tarpon caught in a season was always a great event in the town.

One day he wanted to go up the river in our electric launch. We only had about four mullet for bait, just about enough for one person. So, accompanied by a friend, I volunteered to stay behind in a small boat, try to catch more mullet. I threw mullet bait out on my line and settled down to read a book with the line across the gunnel and then going through my fingers. Pretty soon the line started out fast, then faster and faster. When I braked the line, a big tarpon jumped and tailwalked across the water. After a struggle, we gaffed the tarpon alongside our little cedar rowboat, its head out of the water. I settled down to read again and to wait for the electric launch to pick us up.

Suddenly the fish gave a mighty final gasp. The gaff and my pole went into the water. The boat almost upset, but fortunately the line was under my arm and, after a brief scare, the tarpon was subdued, half-dead by that time.

About then the launch appeared coming down the river, her flags flying, and with father standing on the bow and laughing at me as he shouted, "I got a tarpon! I got a tarpon!'"

It was a little one, only ten pounds, whereas mine weighed 110 pounds.

Charles turned to his father and said: "Don't laugh. Wait till you see what I caught."

Thomas then turned to Fred Ott, who was operating the launch, and said disgustedly,

"Throw mine overboard."

But Ott, for once, wouldn't obey orders. After all, it was his boss's first tarpon. Said Charles,

"We had them both mounted and hung them on a wall facing one of the side verandas at Seminole Lodge. Father—in a friendly way—was always chagrined that I had beaten him. It was a family joke for years."[28]

A list of "Tarpon Record for 1904" in the *Fort Myers Press* states that on March 25, Thomas A. Edison caught a forty-pound tarpon and Charles Edison a one-hundred-pound one. Thus in his taped memoirs Charles slightly underestimated the achievement of his father.[29]

Animals and Plants

Edison was not an animal lover. He had no pets such as dogs or cats, but he shared Mina's interest in birds, and he liked bees because they produced wax, a material that could be used in his experiments and the development of new products. He did not like horses. Once a reporter asked him: "Are you fond of horses?" He answered:

"No. I think they're a poor factor. They're a necessary evil."

Edison was no hunter, and he disliked killing animals. When on nature trips with his friends he did not participate in their shooting activities. On these trips Edison was not physically active as were Henry Ford and Harvey Firestone. Besides watching the general scene and meditating, he busied himself collecting rocks in hope of finding useful minerals and picking wildflowers, which he asked John Burroughs to identify. A companion reported: "Edison, the man whose life is centered in his laboratory, is nevertheless both interested and educated in the myriad wonders of nature. Birds, flowers, stones, he knows them and their secrets."

In Fort Myers Edison had time to watch animals, and he spoke of one such excursion with evident enjoyment in the spring of 1924 about watching the birds and other teeming life about him while the North was still frozen. "But you have to watch out for rattlers," he concluded. "They have big fellows down here, four feet long and as thick as my upper arm. If one of these fellows bites you, you're gone."

"Did you ever hear of a rattlesnake bite proving fatal?" he was asked.

"Yes, sir," Edison answered.

"Now out West where they have thousands of these little fellows, the cowboys don't pay much attention to them. They will flick them with their long squirts just to hear them buzz. Their fangs don't go in far, and there are remedies both internal and external for the bite. But down in Florida the breed is different. They are big ugly fellows with fangs over an inch long. They will puncture right through to an artery and then nothing can save you. I know of a man down there who stepped back—this way—to get a better shot at a bird, and a rattler bit him, and he was dead in four minutes."[30] Despite the threat of snakes, however, he did not try to kill them.

Edison once had an unusual pet in Florida: a raccoon that bit him in the hand so he could not fish. Mina wrote to Charles:

"Papa is as happy as the day is long down here, absolutely loafing! This coon that he has just bought will be quite a pet for him!" And later: "Father and I are out on the pier where it is cool and delightful while inside it is 86°. Father is not fishing as he purchased a coon the other day and when feeding it the bad animal bit him in the hand."[31]

Plants and flowers were Edison's favorite parts of nature. From the very beginning he engaged gardeners to look after his estate. Horticulturists and friends brought him exotic specimens, and today's garden at the Edison estate is a testimony of this hobby. Once Harvey Firestone brought him a specimen of the huge banyan tree that now grows outside the rubber laboratory.

Both Thomas and Mina were very much concerned about the environment around them. Fort Myers sometimes is referred to as the City of Palms because of the magnificent royal palms lining the streets. In 1907 Edison wrote to the town authorities offering to plant palm trees on both sides of Riverside Drive (now McGregor Boulevard), the main road connecting the city with the beaches. He would bring the palms from Cuba, pay for them, plant them, erect crates to protect them, furnish fertilizer and humus, and replace any trees that died—provided the city would promise perpetual care thereafter.[32]

After some initial problems, the royals arrived and thrived. Edison was very fond of the trees by the side of the white fence enclosing Seminole Lodge and his adjoining "rubber plantations" on both sides of the street. He insisted that the palings of the fence be fitted out around the leaning palm trunks because "men should work with nature, rather than try to change nature to their ways."

Conservationists

The south Florida environment first began to be damaged by humans in 1882, when Hamilton Disston, a Philadelphia entrepreneur, brought his dredges up the Caloosahatchee River in an attempt to drain the Everglades and Lake Okeechobee. At the time, everybody including Edison was optimistic about Florida's future not only as a health spa but also as a center of agriculture and new enterprise.

In 1905 the ambitious Napoleon Bonaparte Broward, candidate for governor of Florida, ran on the promise that "the empire of the Everglades" could be drained for a dollar an acre. He had a far-reaching program to drain the Everglades and reclaim vast areas of fertile muckland around Lake Ockeechobee for farming.[33] A former steamboat owner on the East Coast, he also wanted to promote shipping by digging navigable canals crisscrossing the Everglades from Lake Okeechobee to both coasts and dredging a connection north to the St. Johns River. The dredges cut through the green meanders of the winding, spectacular Caloosahatchee River, destroying water oaks and cypress trees and transforming it into a sterile straight canal. Broward's scheme was a move to promote his political ambitions, and it resulted in an environmental disaster. The land that had been drained was prone to flooding.

Later unscrupulous land sharks such as Richard Bolles lured thousands of innocent investors to the still submerged lands of the Everglades. He claimed to be selling a "tropical paradise, richer than the Nile Valley," "the Promised land," and "the poor man's paradise."[34]

In the early 1900s environmental conservation was mostly limited to protection of wild animals, particularly birds and woodlands. Shortsighted economic considerations dominated decision making. "Clearing a forest was a public offence, but draining a marsh or swamp was a public duty." Swamps still evoked fear of contagious diseases, and they were considered "a waste of nature's economy." Drainage purportedly would turn useless wetlands into farmland and forests and beautify the landscape. "Forest conservation meant the maintenance and management of timber stands to achieve a sustained yield of wood products, soil protection, and flood control; swampland policy meant drainage pure and simple."[35]

Mina convinced her husband to change his views on nature. Her activities provided an important forum for the growing conservationist movement not only in Florida but also in New Jersey and New York State. Over the years she attracted many outstanding speakers such as the naturalist and newspaper cartoonist Jay Norwood "Ding" Darling to Chautauqua, New York. Darling also was a friend of Theodore Roosevelt and Herbert Hoover and became increasingly involved in conservationist issues. Later he came to Florida, bought a place on Sanibel Island, and was instrumental in creating a national wildlife refuge there that became the home of many colorful birds such as the roseate spoonbill. He was a frequent visitor to Seminole Lodge.

At an interview in 1925 Edison said he did not think that any inventions could improve Florida. His message was an attempt to stop the massacre of birds and to develop the state's natural beauties and resources. During his drives through Florida, he had noticed with sorrow the denuded forests and the charred stumps of stately pine trees. He had watched the diminution of Florida's beautiful birds as a result of the insensible lust for blood of the "sportsmen" who had driven out the flamingos and hunted the egret heron to virtual extinction.[36] The Edisons probably had the same opinion about wildlife conservation as their friend Allen Andrews, who said: "Most of our conservation today gets no farther than conversation, being largely a fad among social aspirants. It is a subject much like the weather of which Mark Twain once remarked: 'Everybody talks about it, but nobody does anything about it.'"[37]

In later years Thomas and Mina realized that their refuge in southern Florida was threatened by ruthless exploitation. They saw the rich wildlife dwindle, especially after the big property boom in the 1920s and intense road building. Millions of people came to Florida, first by train but later mostly by automobile. In 1928 the seemingly impenetrable Everglades were crossed after blasting with dynamite through sawgrass and cypress swamps, thus creating the Tamiami Trail (U.S. Route 41), the first highway linking the Atlantic and the Gulf from Tampa to Miami. It was an ambitious project that caught the public's fancy.

Road building had begun in 1915 but was abandoned during World War I. Not only did the swampland create an obstacle to the project, but unexpected opposition arose to the northern connecting road between Fort Myers and Punta Gorda. Finally this section was completed with the opening of a bridge across the Caloosahatchee River in 1924. The narrow wooden structure was the first bridge at Fort Myers until the completion of a concrete bridge in October 1930. This new bridge, named Edison Bridge in honor of

Thomas A. Edison, was dedicated on February 11, 1931, on the inventor's eighty-fourth birthday, and the ribbon was cut by Edison himself.

Theodore Edison, the youngest son of Mina and Thomas, was an outspoken conservationist and an active member of the Audubon Society. In *A Plea for Wilderness* he said: "If you value unspoilt nature, you had better speak out now. I have been fortunate enough to have been able to visit many wild places, from the Everglades of Florida to the mountains of Alaska, when those places were really wild, and it saddens me to think that within the past few years a substantial number of the most beautiful and interesting places that I saw have been developed and 'improved' that no one from future generations will be able to get the same deep and lasting impressions that I gained there from seeing both the peaceful and 'violent' grandeur as God made it."[38]

Wet Wonderland

In Florida the conservation movement started early, and in 1905 the Everglades were considered one of the natural wonders of America: "Their mystery is part of our national inheritance. . . . It has its place among the country's native wonders like the Mammoth Cave and Niagara Falls. . . . After all, it is rather a good thing to have a little wonderland left."[39]

These ideas did not come from local politicians but from influential south Florida winter residents of Palm Beach and Miami. The Edisons soon became keen supporters of conservation. Mina Edison was a fervent member of the National Audubon Society, which was instrumental in protecting endangered birds, and she actively tried to fight the extinction of the white egret, herons, and roseate spoonbills. She also supported the Florida Federation of Women's Clubs. Both of these organizations actively promoted the establishment of the Royal Palm State Park forty-five miles southwest of Miami in the middle of the Everglades. At the time the area still was home to 140 different kinds of birds, rare butterflies, tropical snails, and 260 varieties of plants.

Mina and her friends wanted the plants and animals in this area to be saved, and they asked the state to set aside land as a state park. The park was given to the Florida Federation of Women's Clubs in 1915, and Thomas Edison made a cash contribution.[40] Inaugurated the following year, it became the forerunner of the Everglades National Park. Saving alligators and wading birds was, however, not high on the congressional agenda and so officially the park was not established until 1947. The long delay probably could be explained by the fact that the attraction of the Everglades is not obvious to everybody. James Redford is quoted as saying:

> This kind of park is very, very hard to preserve. It is not the sort of national park that generates great public enthusiasm. Some 1.3 million visitors passed through the Everglades' gates in 1968, but it is doubtful that a quarter of them were impressed by the scenery, as is nearly everyone who visits such parks as Yellowstone or Yosemite.
>
> Everglades is a biological park. Its drama is to be found in the spectacular display of wading birds, alligators, fish. For the trained observer it is a living laboratory in which one can see how things fit together in nature. But to the uneducated eye, most of the daily drama of plant and animal dynamics goes unnoticed. In consequence, the cheering section for the Everglades National Park is skimpy.[41]

Theodore Edison commented wisely on the importance of nature reserves:

> There seems to be an almost universal tendency to measure the value of a wild area in terms of the number of people who visit it each year, without taking into account the quality of the experience each visitor obtains, and without making any allowance for the values that do not depend on the presence of any visitor whatsoever. A lonely marsh may serve as a breeding-ground for birds that move to other places and give recurring pleasure to countless people who may not even know that the marsh exists. — The time to act is now — we are rushing toward deadlines marked "too late."[42]

A more spectacular project to create a national park is the sad story of the Big Cypress Swamp. Edison's good friend Henry Ford also was an enthusiastic proponent of the idea of nature conservation and in 1922, before the Lee Tidwater Cypress Logging Company had done away with the remaining giant bald cypress trees in Collier County, he was about to purchase the Big Cypress Swamp and give it to the state of Florida as a nature park. The state declined the generous offer, saying it could not afford roads and maintenance for the park. Finally, in the early 1950s, when most of the giant cypress had been destroyed, the Corkscrew Cypress Rookery Association was formed to preserve the only virgin stand of cypress left in southwest Florida.[43] Money was raised from several sources, and one supporter of the project was Theodore Edison.

Thomas Edison always supported Mina's activities in the conservationist movement even if he did not engage in it himself. When in 1925 Edison was interviewed, he was asked what Florida needed, and he said, "Florida needs absolutely nothing except development. God has given this country everything else, and development will undoubtedly come and is, in fact, already coming very rapidly. Florida's heavenly sunshine is, and always will be, the state's greatest asset. Florida climate is all you need to advertise. While the people in the North are suffering from bronchitis, pneumonia, and other winter ills, here we are in Florida basking in glorious summer sunshine in the winter time." Then came the famous statement: "There is only one Florida—and there are 100,000,000 people up there in the cold who are going to find it out. You don't need anything down here that you haven't already got—but you should conserve what you have. Prevent the fires. Preserve the trees. Protect the birds and keep on developing. When the trees go, the birds will follow suit." Here Mina interrupted: "There is already too much development in my estimation."

At the end, the reporter made an important comment: "The esthetic side of Mr. Edison's character has not previously been stressed, it seems to me. We have heard a lot about his inventions, his questionnaires, his theories about immorality, and his advocacy of four hour's sleep. But his love of the beautiful in nature has been subordinated to his extraordinary inventive genius. It is interesting to know that Mr. Edison does not think any invention can improve Florida's charms. During his trips he has noticed with sorrow the denuded forests, and the diminution of Florida's beautiful birds, the insensate lust for blood of the 'sportsman' who has driven out the flamingo, hunted the aigrette heron to virtual extinction, and is now trying to exterminate every bird left. The 'sportsman' point with pride to their records of 'Fifteen thousand quail killed in a single season.'"[44]

The Edisons would no doubt have been suspicious of many of the projects that today threaten the Everglades such as Wayne Huizenga's twenty-three-hundred-acre Blockbuster Park entertainment complex planned in an area that is home to a wood stork colony and other endangered wetland species.

He found concrete nearly as intriguing as electricity.
JOHN SEDGWICK, 1991

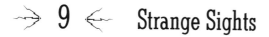 **9** **Strange Sights**

At Seminole Lodge there is a swimming pool made of concrete. It is significant because it was built in 1910 and therefore is one of the first such structures in Florida. Moreover, it is significant for Edison and his diversified activities at that time.

Pioneer in Concrete

In 1902, after abandoning an unsuccessful and costly magnetic ore mining adventure in the hills of New Jersey, Edison decided to use his experience to grind rock into cement rather than iron ore. He would make it from sand and limestone. It was his ambition to produce Portland cement on a large scale and to make a better product at lower cost.

Edison had always been obsessed with using new natural and man-made materials and therefore was fascinated by concrete. John Sedgwick in his article about concrete correctly remarked: "He found it nearly as intriguing as electricity."[1] In 1926 Edison issued a promotional book entitled *The Romance of Cement*.[2] He optimistically believed that it could be used to build structures as solid as the Egyptian pyramids, remarking: "Wood will rot, stone will chip and crumble, bricks disintegrate, but a cement and iron structure is apparently indestructible. Look at some of the old Roman baths. They are still as solid as when they were built."[3]

Concrete was strong, durable, and useful for mass production, and when poured into fancy molds the obedient slurry could be formed in any desired pattern. Edison did not pretend to be artistic and had no qualms about using artificial material such as concrete instead of wood in the construction of complete houses or even phonograph cabinets. Edison's view was contrary to that of the "Victorian communist" John Ruskin, who called concrete "artificial stone" because of its lifeless surface. Edison surely would have loved to use PVC (hardened plastic) had it been available then.

Edison decided to turn to cement manufacture so as to use his equipment and know-how about crushing and grinding ore for a similar technique. The lessons learned in the ore-crushing plant were successfully applied to a novel industry at New Village, where cement rock had been discovered. This was near Stewardsville, only forty-five miles west of his home in West Orange. Here Edison designed a new plant using the large mills from the ore plant to crush the quarried rock. He constructed a giant, 150-foot electric rotary kiln—the first of its kind to be built—which was powerful enough to break a five-ton rock with the ease of a nutcracker and devour fifteen tons of rock every four minutes.[4] The procedure was streamlined so that whereas previously the cement rock was proportioned by wheelbarrows, he now had containers and automatic scales for control. From these formidable works came the 180,000 bags of Edison Portland cement that built the great Yankee Stadium in New York City. Most of the Panama Canal was built with Edison's new product. His cement was also used to build bridges for Flagler's Atlantic Coast Line to Key West, and in Havana, Cuba, it was employed for large apartment buildings.

Avant-Garde Builder

In 1907 Edison constructed his garage and a gardener's cottage at West Orange from a precast iron mold into which cement was poured. These buildings were so successful that in the following year he decided to work with concrete for mass production of houses. The New York Press termed it "cosy houses for working men" "cast-in-one-piece."[5] Pipes, sinks, and electrical conduits, bathtubs, and ceiling ornamentation were set in place in the mold and cast into the house. Even concrete furniture could be ordered to complete the decor, and a special jelly was mixed with the cement to give it a woodlike appearence. Some people, however, were skeptical: "This idea is one of the insanities of genius. Edison is crazy. He wouldn't be a great inventor if he were not."[6]

But Edison was in good company—he was the predecessor of the famous avant-garde European architects Le Corbusier and Gropius, who in the 1920s enthusiastically embraced the idea of large-scale mass-production techniques. Le Corbusier proposed that natural materials be replaced with artificial components and suggested that houses made of concrete poured into forms could be completed in three days.[7]

Florida's Most Famous Pool

In 1910, before he left Fort Myers to go to New Jersey, Edison instructed Harvey Heitman, his caretaker, to construct a concrete swimming pool on his lot near the Caloosahatchee River. He would combine Portland cement, shells, and cinders, reinforced with woven steel wire. The contractor was William Wallace, who charged the large sum of $665 for constructing the pool, including water pipes, plank walk, fence, and dressing rooms, all neatly painted. The "bathing pool" was ready in November, but when the water was let in, the pool drained because the riverside wall was leaking. Therefore, the walls had to be reinforced with rocks and more concrete.[8] The pool still stands and has never required repairs. Next to Ernest Hemingway's pool built in 1937 at his house in Key West it is Florida's most famous on-land private bathing facility.

The real pioneer of concrete buildings and swimming pools in Florida, however, was Henry Flagler, the railroad king of the East Coast. Both of his hotels in St. Augustine, the ostentatious Ponce de Leon and the Alcazar, built in 1887, were made of concrete. These monolithic structures, inspired by Spanish and Italian Renaissance styles, were constructed of cast concrete, composed of six parts of coquina shell and one part cement. David Chandler described the building process: "When the pouring of cement became a problem, Flager had his agents recruit 1,200 Negroes from the countryside and brought them to stamp the liquid coquina gravel into the wooden construction forms with their bare feet while musicians played lively music." One of the Alcazar's more splendid features was a 120-foot-long swimming pool, divided into separate sections for ladies and gentlemen. Flagler wanted any conceivable luxury possible and installed four Edison direct current dynamos to provide electric lighting for the hotels and his private villa.[9]

The Hollow Sphere

In 1894 a strange neighbor moved to the Gulf Coast: Dr. Cyrus Teed. A former medical practitioner, Teed came from wind-blown Chicago to Estero not far from Fort Myers. He was a sturdy man with piercing eyes and unusual ideas who called himself "Koresh." He wanted to build his own empire, a new Jerusalem, and founded the Koreshan Unity Colony in balmy Florida, expecting to attract millions of followers. Skeptics called him a crackpot.

Teed had received a vision: the earth is a hollow globe with the sun, the moon, and all the stars contained inside. According to Teed, we did not live on the outside but on the inside of the twenty-five-thousand-mile circumference. He and his followers conducted "geodesic" experiments on the beaches of Naples to prove his theory, and he proposed the concept of "cellular cosmogeny" in which he reasoned that "all life develops from cellular forms. Nature is uniform, life in the aggregate must conform to the same general laws. The Universe must conform." Initially he brought with him thirty followers who had given up all their private possessions thinking that the love of money was the root of all evil. Eventually about two hundred people decided to turn over everything they owned to the society. They built dormitories, one for men and another for women. The Koreshans practiced celibacy as recommended by their leader, who by this time was on in years and already had children. The community was practically a complete unit within itself, made up of people from all walks of life. They operated a sawmill and a bakery and eventually started their own electrical plant, which was shut down at bedtime, nine o'clock every evening. There also was a general store, a carpenter shop, and fruit and vegetable plantations, and they published their own newspaper, the *American Eagle*. The Koreshans, unlike many other radical sectarians, were kind and peaceful people who lived in a world of their own, reading and studying, and the colony developed into a center of culture, with music, and drama. They built an art hall where a fifteen-piece orchestra and brass band played. They also organized carnivals and pageants in the spacious park grounds that were attended by a large number of people from Fort Myers and Lee County.[10] Dr. Teed and his followers were unmercifully castigated by the local and national press: "Teed is not the first rascal who has made religion a cloak for his designs against the property and personal liberty of others."[11]

In 1908 Dr. Teed died, but his followers carried on. The remaining members of the colony lived in a simple fashion. They farmed and fished and lived exemplary lives, and one of them, Allen Andrews, became a friend of the Edisons because of his interest in nature and gardening. He was the editor of the *American Eagle*, which eventually became one of the best horticultural papers in the country.

In 1914 Edison, Ford, and Burroughs visited the colony. They enjoyed the plantation and buildings but thought that the people "had a screw loose somewhere."[12]

Old John Burroughs was perplexed by the religious creed of these educated people who believed that they lived on the inside of the globe: "In a secluded place we found a religious sect, embracing men and women of culture and refinement, who upheld the social and civic virtues and cultivated the industrial arts, yet who deemed it essential for their soul's salvation to disbelieve all our popular astronomy, and hold to the idea that, instead of living on the outside of a globe, we live inside a hollow sphere. These Florida fanatics defy common sense and the exact demonstrations of science."[13]

It must be said, however, that John Burroughs at times found it difficult to imagine that he lived on top of a sphere: "I am turned topsy-turvy every time I try to see myself on a round globe. I fancy that all persons who think much about the matter have trouble to adjust their notion of a round world to their actual experience."[14]

The last member of the Koreshan Unity Colony, Hedwig Michel, from Germany, died at the age of ninety in 1982. Dr. Teed's settlement at Estero now is the Koreshan State Park.[15]

Everything has turned to rubber in our family.
We talk rubber, think rubber, dream rubber.

MINA EDISON, 1927

→ 10 ← Rubber and Goldenrod

In 1927 Edison lost interest in the day-to-day running of his business empire and invention factory. He was relieved to hand over responsibility to his son Charles. But even in old age Edison could not sit idle. He wanted something new, but what? Maybe he felt like the lonely and puzzled character Aladdin, depicted in a contemporary cartoon, who, surrounded by all the marvelous achievements of the century, was looking at the wonderlamp of invention and saying sadly, "I wish—I wish I had sump'n to wish for."

Rubber on the Mind

When on their second voyage Christopher Columbus and his followers reached the Caribbean Islands, they were mesmerized by watching Haitians play with bouncing balls made of tree gum. Obviously, these natives had recognized the peculiar properties of the dried milky juice of some tropical trees. That was the Western world's first encounter with what the American Indians called *cahuchu*, a term the French transformed into *caoutchouc*.

The practical-minded English learned that the sticky stuff they brought from their eastern colonies could be used instead of bread crumbs to rub out black-lead pencil marks and called it India rubber. Soon other uses were found for rubber. In rainy Scotland the inventive Charles Macintosh created waterproof fabrics by dipping them in rubber dissolved in turpentine. In 1838 Charles Goodyear added sulfur and invented the vulcanization process, which converted the sticky material into a durable elastic mass for shoes, hoses, and carriage wheels. The first commercial rubber was obtained by the British from *Ficus elastica*—the original India rubber tree, now grown as an ornamental pot plant. After 1880 the principal source of rubber, however, became the hevea tree (*Hevea brasiliensis*), a member of the *euphorbiacae* and native of central South American tropical jungles. In 1876 the British brought seeds of the tree to London and raised saplings in the greenhouse at Kew Gardens. From there they distributed the hevea tree to their colonies in the Far East. It was soon successfully planted in India, Malaysia, and Ceylon. The hevea tree yields much larger quantities and better-quality rubber than conventional "rubber trees" and soon became the source of the world supply of rubber.

During Edison's lifetime rubber became an increasingly important commodity in the Western industrialized world. After 1890, with the introduction of fast-moving wheels, pneumatic tires for bicycles and automobiles became available. At that point the rubber industry expanded explosively and so did the demand for the raw material.

It may seem strange that Edison, who was so interested in chemistry, took the old-fashioned approach of hunting for plants as source of rubber. But plantation rubber from hevea trees in the Far East had only recently been introduced, and by this time Edison was too old to venture into the new field of synthetic chemistry.

Rubber production on a large scale was Edison's last project. Research on a new natural source of rubber was a departure from his previous line of laboratory work, totally unrelated to electricity, phonographs, or movies. He did not continue development of the radio because he felt distanced from the innovations of wireless and electronic communication. Edison's increasing deafness reinforced his preference for the tangible and visible instead of the abstract and invisible. Thus he did not pursue the new, promising line of synthetic rubber research, instead looking for a new natural source by collecting latex-producing plants and mounting dried specimens of them on herbarium cards.

Edison's rubber project in Florida was concentrated on extracting the substance from natural sources. When Ford in 1927 sent him a sample of synthetic rubber, he was quoted as replying: "All synthetic rubber is made from materials that must be grown. All the big chemists in Germany, England and in this country are unanimous in stating that synthetic rubber cannot compete with tree rubber at forty cents."[1]

In reality, Edison's interest in rubber was not new. He had always been interested in it because he needed both hard and soft rubber for many of his experimental projects. In 1895 an article in the *Chemical Industry Journal* reported that Edison was working on producing imitation rubber from vegetable fibers, and in 1888 he conducted experiments to find a substitute for hard rubber. In 1904 he said: "I am thinking of putting up a small plant to make hard rubber parts for my new storage battery."

The first seeds of the new project were sown in 1915 when Ford, Firestone, and Edison visited the Panama-Pacific Exposition in California and went to see Luther Burbank, the "wizard of plants," at his farm in Santa Rosa. The idea of producing domestic rubber was again on Edison's mind, and he suggested to his friends that a method should be developed for production of natural rubber from a domestic plant that could easily be grown and harvested in the United States. Edison clearly realized that in case of emergency a large-scale domestic supply of rubber would be vital even if the cost of production was high. He said: "The United States requires an independent rubber supply, easily accessible. We all hope that we shall never see another war. But suppose we do, and our rubber supply is far overseas, in foreign hands? Modern armies—future armies—will travel on rubber. Every need of our times demands rubber. So I am trying to assure a domestic supply of war rubber for the United States—if the time should come when it is needed. Yes, that is my greatest problem now."

But what plant could yield enough latex from its leaves or stem? Attempts at domestic production had been made earlier, but no substitute had yet been found for the hevea tree. Some American plants and trees yielded a rubbery sap but not enough for industrial production.

Burbank was famous for mass production of sensational new plant hybrids. In Santa Rosa this self-taught, hardworking man had created wonderful new fruits such as white blackberries and stoneless prunes. He had also been very successful in creating new varieties of potatoes and flowers by hybridization, that is, crossing related varieties and species to produce new types. Later he experimented with cacti, hoping to get rid of their spines so they could be used for animal fodder in the desert. Edison was greatly impressed by Burbank's success at growing new flowers and shrubs with improved qualities. There seemed to be no limit to the improvements that could be made with plants by cross-breeding and selection. He thought, "If Burbank can do it I can do it too, I will be able to grow new plants with a higher rubber content."

When Edison in 1930 was asked about his method to improve upon the rubber content of his goldenrod plants, he talked about the different species, how he had cultivated them and crossbred them through various stages and in different ways to improve their sap-producing qualities. He added with a chuckle: "I am trying to take Burbank's place."

It was thought that there was no native goldenrod in Florida, but plants of unusual size had been found in Polk County, and Edison used these to develop his own species, which were over 12 feet long. When asked about the rubber content in plants other than goldenrod, he answered, "While many other plants had a somewhat higher content of rubber-producing juices, they were utterly impracticable as a 'growable and movable crop,'" and their manufacture would be far more complicated and expensive."

Rubber Crisis

The postwar boom in auto manufacture in the 1920s led by Henry Ford brought self-propelled wheels to the American public and caused an ever-increasing demand for rubber, especially after the introduction of balloon tires in 1923. The United States consumed more than 70 percent of the world rubber harvest, and eight out of every ten pounds went into automobile tires. Harvey Firestone was a market leader in tire production. Already, in 1924, the government through the influence of Firestone introduced a program that aimed to make the United States independent of foreign rubber. The Department of Agriculture built a $100,000 plant introduction station at Chap-man Field, 20 miles south of Miami, where experiments were being conducted with various kinds of rubber plants. Edison, Ford, and Firestone kept in close contact with the work at this station.

A shortage of natural rubber was expected after the British introduced a rubber restriction act in hope of improving sales of a commodity from the British colonies, which dominated the market. The act was masterminded in London by the colonial secretary, Winston Churchill, who said: "It should be the cause of great satisfaction to us, being the principal means of paying our debt to the United States."[2]

Henry Ford was fed up with the British-Dutch rubber monopoly. Having mastered the production of cars, he now wanted to try to control the raw material that went into cars, rubber and steel. Ford began his quest for rubber near his winter home in Florida. He had acquired eight thousand acres of land in the vicinity of La Belle, not far from Fort Myers, and in 1925 it was reported that "his representatives set out some 500 imported rubber trees on a certain test plot in this great area. The trees seemed to be coming along satisfactorily in the soil of their adoption when all of a sudden the floods engendered by the excessive rainfall of last autumn swept over the planted area and drowned out all experimental trees."[3]

In 1927 Ford began a new project in Brazil to grow rubber trees. Firestone had started a hevea plantation in Liberia in 1924. Ford's Brazilian venture failed, but Firestone eventually succeeded in getting trees in Africa to produce rubber. At this time Firestone and Ford became increasingly disturbed by the problem of the source of rubber and approached Edison with the idea of starting production from alternative natural sources. The two men believed in Edison's great ablities and also were eager to inspire the ailing man by encouraging him to do the only thing he really loved: working hard to invent new things. Therefore, when Edison agreed to conduct exhaustive plant research in Florida for the development of natural rubber, his friends were overjoyed. In 1927 Edison, Firestone, and Ford decided to start a joint venture to produce domestic rubber, which became the Edison Botanic Research Corporation of Fort Myers, Florida. The principal objective of the company was "to carry on and conduct experimental and research work relating to the production of rubber, from vegetation and to make objects either in whole or part from rubber. The corporation may also engage in wholesale merchandising and export and import of products."[4]

Firestone and Ford each advanced $93,500, and Edison contributed his laboratory, labor, and know-how.[5] Their objective was not necessarily to find a source of rubber that could be economically competitive with the production in tropical countries but to ensure a supply of domestic rubber in an emergency.

At the time, a large number of mostly imported ficus or rubber trees were growing in Florida but only two native species, the strangler fig, *Ficus aurea*, and the poplar-leaved fig, *Ficus populnea*. The former is a common tree in Florida hammocks. It grows on the limbs of other trees from seeds dropped by birds and gradually chokes its host to death by sending air roots to the ground. These roots yield a white sap containing latex when the tree is injured.

These sources, however, were not practical. Why not grow the real thing, the Brazilian hevea, in Florida? Attempts had been made before (Henry Ford had tried to grow the tree), but the climate was not conducive for the full-grown tree. In 1840 Charles Goodyear, the pioneer in rubber processing, tried to plant rubber trees in Florida. Together with Henry Perrine he organized the Florida Tropical Plant Company. In 1924 new attempts were made to raise rubber in Florida after Congress appropriated money for experimental domestic production. Promoters of the venture were optimistic, and the public opinion as expressed by a magazine was that "it is not a far cry to visualize potential rubber factories in the land of palm trees and sunshine converting homegrown rubber into important articles of commerce."[6]

Seedlings of rubber plants were raised at the Chapman Experimental Station near Coconut Grove. But it soon became evident that even if it was possible to grow hevea in Florida, it would probably not be profitable in a land where labor was scarce and expensive because rubber is extracted by manual tapping, that is, collecting latex from incisions in the bark, the sap flowing into a small receptacle placed on the trunk. The Florida plants, however, had the advantage that they were free from diseases that attack them in other parts of the world. Therefore, these young rubber trees were mainly produced for export to the West Indies to be used in the development of new rubber plantations there.[7]

In the early 1920s Edison experimented with different milky-juiced plants such as *Guayule*, a silver-leafed Mexican shrub of which he had obtained some samples from Firestone. Initially, in 1923, Edison enthusiastically wrote to Ford with a plan: "I find that the bushes average twenty-four inches high, they occupy a horizontal space of about one foot, and probably grow 40,000 bushes to an acre. They give 7.5 grams of good rubber per bush. This would give 680 pounds of rubber per acre, worth $183. I think that there will be no trouble to reap or plant with machinery."[8]

Further investigations, however, were disappointing and revealed that *Guayule* is a slow-growing woody shrub that must grow for four to five years before latex can be harvested from it. Edison was not alone in his search for a new source of domestic rubber, and *Guayule* had already been exploited on a commercial basis by a capitalist with vision: Bernard Baruch, who worked with the Intercontinental Rubber Company in the southwestern United States.[9]

Edison also tried the seeds of the *Carissa* bush, which he obtained from the Everglades Nursery. Ultimately, however, he was not looking for new rubber trees or bushes. He wanted a low native plant that could be grown rapidly, preferably yielding more than one crop a year, and that could be harvested and processed on a large scale by use of machinery. He said: "My experiments are all aimed at finding a plant prolific enough to produce a crop of rubber in 18 months in time of war."[10]

Once on the way back from visiting Ford in Detroit, he stopped his car several times and picked plants he thought might be useful for his rubber experiments. The giant milkweed attracted his attention. He wrote to Ford: "It grows all along the road on which I came back to Orange, except I saw none in limestone soils. There I found another variety resembling the giant but it's not so high. I also saw two other kind of milk weed plants." In 1923 Edison had done experiments with the *Asclepias* milkweeds, perennial herbs of which there are twelve varieties in America. These plants are noted for their milky sap, which could be a source of rubber. He became particularly interested in the giant milkweed.

By 1925 his interest shifted to *Cryptostegia grandiflora*, a Madagascar vine with a milky juice of high rubber content. It had the advantage of growing vigorously in south Florida and when young could be harvested with machinery. Edison thought this to be a promising shrub and asked Ford to set up a pilot plantation at his Fort Thompson farm, upriver from Fort Myers. But following several attempts, he eventually gave up because he could not figure out how to extract the rubber in commercial quantities.

The Quest for Rubber

In 1927 serious rubber research began in Fort Myers but later was carried out simultaneously at West Orange and in Florida. The first experiments were done in Edison's original electric laboratory on the riverside near the Edison winter home. In November 1927 carloads of new laboratory equipment were sent to Fort Myers, and when the aged inventor arrived in January 1928, he immediately started work with a team of seven men, a chief chemist and six botanists. He also engaged the famous botanist John Kunkel Small of the New York Botanical Garden, the foremost authority on the flora of the southeastern United States. Small spent a month in Florida helping Edison's team in their research on rubber plants.

When in June of 1928 the old lab was dismantled and shipped to Dearborn, Michigan, all the paraphernalia used for rubber experiments was transferred to a new lab across McGregor Boulevard. The new rubber laboratory is a long green building with many windows which was erected amid a plantation of rubber plants, flowers, and trees. The green building still stands and is now overshadowed by the huge banyan rubber tree planted by Harvey Firestone in 1925.

As always, Edison started his work systematically. His way of attacking the problem was described by men who knew him personally. His secretary, William Henry Meadowcraft, explained:

> With his accustomed thoroughness, he is ransacking the world for every bit of information he can obtain in regard to rubber and its cultivation and manufacture. The books he has so far read would fill two five-foot bookshelves, to say nothing of domestic and foreign magazines and periodicals devoted to the subject. Mr. Edison has undertaken a stupendous task. However, he glories in it, and has attacked the problem with his old-time completeness, vigor and enthusiasm. I have never seen him *more* thoroughly wrapped up in and concentrated on any of his investigations.[11]

Another friend described the process of searching for the right plant:

> His success depended largely on his physical make-up, as well as certain solidity of his nervous system that takes no account of fatigue or ennui. In other words, day after day, with only a few hours' sleep he can devote himself enthusiastically to the investigation of a single problem, the very monotony of which could drive most men into nervous prostration. Mr. Edison could go into a field of grass a mile square and select therefrom the most perfect blade! The popular conception of Mr. Edison is that of a man who accomplishes startling results by instantaneous flashes of intellect. The real Edison is a man of *indefatigable* industry, who attains his ends by patient effort intelligently applied.[12]

After the initial experiments on already known sources, he checked thousands of new plants, using the same empirical approach he had when looking for the best carbon filament for his electric lamp half a century earlier. ("People are not remembered by how many times they fail, but how many times they succeed. Every wrong step is another step forward.") He organized a hunt on a massive scale and engaged botanists and laymen in a search covering the southern states as far north as New Jersey. For each plant an herbarium card was made on which the dried specimen was mounted, which was sent to Rutgers University for identification.

In 1928, at the age of eighty-one, when asked what he thought of his new work, Edison happily remarked: "I've had sixty years in physics and mechanics and now I have taken up something entirely different and it is mighty interesting and I am enjoying it."[13] As a boy his life revolved around his chemistry experiments, and now he confessed that such work remained his deepest interest and that he was more of a chemist than a physicist or engineer.[14]

The chemical processing of the specimens included extraction with acetone and other media to remove nonrubber constituents and then extraction with benzene (benzol) to get the "rubbery gunk." Edison himself took an active part in all stages of the work. He looked at the specimens and inspected the dried benzol extracts, making notes on their color and physical properties. It is typical of Edison that he checked every step of the procedure and was concerned with the safety of his fellow workers. Since there was some doubt about the toxicity of benzene, he instructed his technicians to do the extraction outside the laboratory if at all possible and later under a fume hood.[15] Edison instinctively sensed danger and substituted another process for the benzene procedure. His fear was justified for we now know that inhalation of benzene can cause serious blood disease. A similar situation had occurred in 1886, when he stopped working with radium and X rays; he was one of the first researchers to be aware of the dangers of radiation.

Goldenrod

In 1929 there was feverish activity in Fort Myers. One visitor from up north testified: "I am convinced that the Globe is but a rubber ball," and another said, "It was a great joy to meet the new King Midas with the rubber touch and his queen."[16]

In less than a year Edison had checked more than 3,000 indigenous plants, and 1,700 of them were growing in his gardens in Fort Myers. He boasted: "Everything looks favorable to a solution." Ultimately, 14,000 plants were examined and tested. Edison eventually found 1,240 to have some rubber content and then narrowed the field down to 600 that were potentially profitable.[17]

Eventually he selected goldenrod, or *solidago*, as the best choice. It could be harvested like hay by modern machinery, two crops a year, macerated, and put into huge tanks for extracting latex by using a solvent. Goldenrod is a large family of more than 125 species, all but a few native to North America. In New York alone there are thirty varieties. They are perennial erect herbs that stand up to five feet high, with a slender stem, oblong leaves, and yellow flowers.[18] The name *solidago* is derived from the Latin word *solidare*, to unite or heal, because the plant was known as a "vulnerary herb." A variety of goldenrod, *Solidago odora*, once was recognized in the United States Dispensatory as possessing sufficient medical virtues to be recommended not to heal open wounds but to serve as a stimulant and to relieve pain and nausea by using the leaves as a tea.

Influenced by Luther Burbank, Edison did not just accept one solidago species with a high rubber content but set out to hybridize a superior variety through cross-breeding. He cross-pollinated the small goldenrod with a giant variety, fourteen feet tall, from the Everglades. It grew fast and could easily be harvested in the United States. It was later named after Edison, *Solidago edisoni*. A specimen of the giant goldenrod is on display in the chemical laboratory at Fort Myers. Goldenrod was planted in Fort Myers and on Ford's plantation at Fort Thompson. The analytical work was supervised by C. A. Prince, a pharmacist who lived in Fort Myers but moved north with Edison during the summer months. Although the rubber content was not as high as in the sap obtained from the real tropical rubber tree, Ford was so impressed by Edison's reports that he purchased extensive acreage in southern Georgia for raising goldenrod.[19]

Research in hope of extracting rubber from goldenrod occupied Edison until the end of his life. His good friend James Newton tells the story of his final triumph:

> I remember the day he produced crude rubber—from different strains of goldenrod. He discovered that he could get up to 12% natural rubber—enough to make commercial production feasible. Edison had been up at 4:30 that morning, waiting on his porch for enough light to go across to the laboratory, and all day long he worked there and finally achieved his breakthrough.
>
> I went over a little before nine in the evening to help him celebrate by taking him to the movies. The gardener had put up a rope over a square of grass that he was reseeding. As we crossed the lawn in the dark, we ran into this rope, which was chest-high. Edison, who was eighty years old, backed up and kicked his leg way up over the rope— he was so joyful at having produced rubber that day. Then we went to the movies.[20]

In Fort Myers rubber production was kept on an experimental scale. Edison had ten men employed in cutting and stripping the leaves of the tall stalks of *solidago*. He hired W. N. Archer to supervise his goldenrod plantation. As always, Edison was not satisfied with conventional techniques. Together with his trusted assistant, Fred Ott, he developed his own process and machinery for chopping goldenrod and extracting rubber. He obtained one of his last patents (No. 1090) on December 7, 1929, "for the extraction of rubber from plants." In September 1930 the first big crop was shipped to the West Orange laboratories.

After his death in 1931, research continued on a smaller scale until 1935 under the direction of Harry Uckelberg. During this period the botanical work was carried out in Fort Myers and the analytical testing at West Orange. In June 1931, Charles Edison revealed that his father's rubber experiments had passed the preliminary stage and the new rubber had been successfully vulcanized.[21] In 1934 the plots yielded three hundred pounds of rubber per acre and rubber contents as high as 12.4 percent.

Walter Buswell, botanist and onetime assistant in the rubber laboratory at Fort Myers, once was asked why rubber production from goldenrod never developed to the point that it could be of practical value in supplying domestic rubber during an emergency such as World War II. He answered that goldenrod was not a reliable source of raw rubber. The plant might be high in latex content one season, but the following year it might be unsatisfactory. Therefore, one could not expect a fixed percentage of latex from year to year, a prerequisite for industrial production.

Beyond Goldenrod

The rubber project was Edison's last big enterprise using his empirical hunt-and-try approach. Why did the man whose prime interest was chemistry not try to develop a synthetic process? The chemical lab in West Orange, which always had been his *sanctum sanctorum*, would have been the ideal place to do such work. In 1926, when the research started in Florida, no doubt he was well aware that rubber could be produced synthetically, but Edison wanted something different.

As early as 1826 the chemical formula for rubber had been established by his idol in electromagnetics and chemistry, Michael Faraday, but there was still a long way to go. He had studied the pertinent literature in current textbooks and journals such as *Industrial and Engineering Chemistry*, to which he subscribed. In 1926 this journal published a review of all aspects of rubber production, both natural and synthetic.[22]

Some experimental synthesis was first successfully achieved from turpentine and acetylene, but industrial production of synthetic rubber first became a reality in Germany during World War I, when their supply of natural rubber was cut off. This early synthetic rubber was, however, of low quality and far inferior to the natural stuff.

By the time Edison's hunt for rubber plants was completed, new synthetic processes were being developed in the modern factories of DuPont and General Electric. These research laboratories used the scientific approach to developing new materials by theoretical deduction rather than the sweat of trial and error. The successful production of synthetic rubber, neoprene, was announced by the DuPont Company in 1931, the year Edison died, and the first tires made of neoprene were produced by Firestone in 1933.[23]

During World War II, a supply of rubber again became a critical issue, and after Pearl Harbor President Franklin Roosevelt attempted to create a national rubber policy by appointing a committee headed by Bernard Baruch, who had started the *Guayule* project in 1910. The plan called for the production not only of synthetic rubber but also of domestic natural rubber from various plants. Edison's rubber files were examined, and the Emergency Rubber Act listed goldenrod as a possible source. Further research showed that the low-molecular-weight solidago rubber could be blended with synthetic rubber and used to replace up to 20 percent of *hevea* rubber. After World War II synthetic production provided the major supply of rubber both in Europe and America.[24]

A somewhat tragic note in Edison's struggle was that by the time he managed to produce appreciable quantities of rubber, world prices had dropped and there was no immediate need for rubber from goldenrod. Edison was now very sick, but his friends Ford and Firestone did not withdraw their support, partly because they felt sorry for him and were concerned about his well-being.

The end of the story was told by Byron Vanderbilt: "Edison and other members of his party came south on January 12, 1931, and the work continued there. By early spring it was evident that Edison was a very sick man. He was transported in a wheel chair from the porch of his home across McGregor Boulevard to the rubber laboratory where he had a desk and a chair." Edison always gave specific instructions as to what equipment to ship north well before moving day. In 1931 he did not leave Fort Myers until early June, which was one or two months later than usual. As the time of departure came near and still there was no word from Edison, young Prince (who worked on the project) was requested by the laboratory and field personnel to find out what Edison wanted shipped. Prince wrote a note to this effect (Edison was completely deaf by this time) and handed it to him one morning while he was sitting on the porch. He got a one-word answer: 'Everything.' Edison knew that he would never return to Fort Myers."[25]

Today no less than fifteen varieties of rubber trees adorn the garden of the Edison winter home. One of them, the huge Indian banyan ficus tree, nearly covers the entire rubber laboratory, the Green Laboratory. It was planted in 1925 when Edison received it as a present from Harvey Firestone. This tree has a strange life story, starting as an epiphyte. Birds carry the seed to hollow branches of a tree where they germinate to seek shelter high above ground. Then they develop threadlike air roots hanging down to the earth to gain a footing. After that it becomes a terrestrial tree and the air roots grow thick and develop into supporting stems while expanding over a large area. This extremely vital tree in Fort Myers, the largest of its kind in the continental United States, is a living monument to the unsurpassed achievements of a great man of Florida.

Like the bush in the sea near my Florida home, the man,
the cat, the elephant are collections of units.

THOMAS ALVA EDISON, 1920

→ 11 ← Sponges of Life

Edison never troubled himself much with abstract philosophy or the identity of a Supreme Being, but he had a strong feeling for objects he could perceive and classify. Nevertheless, he wanted to find answers to all kinds of questions, not only ones involving electricity. Explanations were necessary to him, and he believed that every theory, every concept, could be boiled down to facts, machinery, and measurable units.

He was always keenly observant of things around him in his work and leisure time, if he ever enjoyed such a thing as leisure. He was immensely interested in biology and nature, not only as sources of raw material for his inventions but as they related to questions of life and death. Particularly in later years, his mind was occupied with religion and the question of whether there was life after death.

When he was working in his laboratory in the North, he faced pressing problems, and time passed swiftly so he rarely had the leisure to pursue thoughts about religion. But when he was in Florida, there was ample opportunity to watch plants and animals and to connect his observations with his theories. Writing in a meticulous and often distinctive calligraphy, he made notes about many things, including nature and immortality as seen from his perspective at Seminole Lodge. At one time the object of his curiosity was sponges, mysterious multicellular animals with a tough supporting framework of fibers. These creatures gave him a strange idea about life which he tried to explain.

Life Entities

In Florida, Edison indulged in boating and fishing. He was not only a meditative angler on the pier of Seminole Lodge, but he made frequent expeditions down the Caloosahatchee River to Punta Rassa and Sanibel Island. During these fishing trips he studied the aquatic life of fishes, mollusks, and multitudes of corals and sponges. Edison was fascinated by sponges because he thought they revealed the fundamental principles of life.

He had become more closely acquainted with sponges in 1918, during World War I, when working for the Naval Consulting Board station in Key West. There nobody could ignore the sponge industry because of the evil smell spreading from the city wharf where the slimy rotting cargo was landed. Next to cigar manufacture, it was the biggest trade product of Key West, used not only in the household as toilet sponges but in surgery for removing blood and checking hemorrhages during operations. Edison was already familiar with sponges because he had used them as insulators in his electrical machines and installations.

At Key West he saw masses of these creatures brought into the harbor by sponge fishers whose schooners operated on the west coast all the way up to Apalachicola. At the time sponging was done from small boats in shallow water. The vessels were first towed astern of a schooner to their destination and then two men jumped into each boat. One stood aft sculling with a long oar, while the other bent low overboard, his head buried in a wooden bucket with a glass bottom eagerly scanning the sea bottom as they slowly moved over it. In clear waters all submerged objects to a depth of thirty to forty feet could be seen: darting fish, branching coral, gorgeous anemones, bristling sea porcupines, and dark, orange, and yellow round or fingerlike objects, the sponges. Upon spotting sponges, the fisherman would reach for a long rake and pull out a dark, slimy mass that he triumphantly pronounced to be a grass sponge. Edison studied the strange creatures, which were an enigma to biologists.

Edison read all about them. In the past most scientists had labeled them as plants, but recently it had become apparent that sponges were primitive animals and that they had an extraordinary ability to regenerate parts of their bodies. Scientists had crushed sponges, strained the soft matter through a cloth, and seen the cells regroup to form another sponge. For a long time this process intrigued Edison, and one day he decided that sponges were a metaphor of creation and it struck him that he had found a clue to life in general:

> Down in Florida, where I have a place, there is a bush which grows in the ocean—that is, it seems to be a bush. Really it is animal matter built into a bush form by the efforts of thousands of insects; it is the work of highly organized individuals massed in a crowd for the purpose of building. A certain class of organized, living beings, large enough even to be seen with the naked eye, builds structures which appear to be but are no plants, being nothing, more or less than swarms of insects gathered in that form in order that they may get food conveniently.
>
> Consider the sponge. It seems vegetable, but is an animal. Investigate it further, and you will find it to be an aggregate which has been built by a group of insects. The uninformed who see it, native whites and negroes, believe this insect-aggregate to be a vegetable individual—a sea-tree.
>
> Almost all men, even those whom we accept as best informed, make similar mistakes with regard to that which we denominate as a man, or a cat, or an elephant. We think the man is a unit, that he is just a man; we think the cat is just a cat; we think the elephant a unit, that is just an elephant.
>
> I am convinced that such thinking is basically in error. Like the "bush" seems to be a unit, an individual. The man does. The cat does. The elephant does. But it is only seeming.
>
> Each is made up of many individuals gathered in a community, and it is the community. The unit which makes it up may be too small even for the microscope to see. Everything we can see is a manifestation of community, not of individual effort.[1]

Molecular Biology

At the time people were very much impressed by the French surgeon Alexis Carrel, who in 1912 had received the Nobel Prize for new techniques to suture blood vessels and the transplantation of organs. Carrel also had managed to grow cells outside the body; he kept these tiniest bits of life replicating for a year in a glass dish. Edison was well aware of Carrel's work as presented in the magazine he helped found, *Science*, and in the *Scientific American*.[2]

Edison believed in the "swarm," or ensemble, of the basic entity of life, more specifically, an assembly of small, microscopic, or even submicroscopic elementary units, like a sponge, that make up the individual organism. He was obsessed with these entities as carriers of life. He once did an experiment to show that the basic life units were capable of reproduction. He injured the skin of his thumb and was able to show that the regrowing skin was in every detail a copy of the original skin with all its folds and crevices. Therefore, the body must be a carrier of templates of reproduction, basic submicroscopic units bearing the characteristics of the body. "I am convinced that the body is made up of entities, which are intelligent. When one cuts his finger I believe it is the intelligence of these entities that heals the wound. When one is sick it is the intelligence of these entities that brings convalescence."[3] Edison's reasoning is remarkable in that it anticipates the DNA gene theory of modern molecular biology.

To Edison the basic life entities were not only the building blocks of a primitive organism such as a sponge or coral but also made up the entire human body, with its memory and soul. Character and personality could be explained by a swarm of entities of memory cells in the fold of Broca, a distinct area in the third convolution of the left frontal lobe of the brain containing neurons controlling speech. It was named for Paul Broca, the French neurologist and anthropologist who studied failures of speech and mapped areas of the brain where damage had caused a specific problem. Edison was much impressed by this discovery, the first indication that specific functions are the province of particular locations of the brain, and, in general terms, that there is a connection between the anatomy of the brain and its function.

Edison's theory of life can be traced back to the turn of the century, when his thoughts often turned to the mysteries of life and matter. At the time, he was convinced that atoms gathered together in certain forms constitute animals and man, "who represents the total intelligence of all atoms."[4] In 1916, when John Burroughs visited the Edisons in Florida, he reported that Edison had spoken about the "monoids," tiny things that regulated the human mental machinery. After their outings to the Everglades, Edison said that his monoids had been "greatly refreshed."[5] His experience with sponges, which led him to formulate his theory of "life entities," followed in 1920.

Edison's view also had much in common with that of his friend Luther Burbank, who professed:

> Every atom, molecule, plant, animal or planet is only an aggregation of organized unit forces, held in place by stronger forces, thus holding them for a time latent, though teeming with inconceivable power.
>
> I prefer and claim the right to worship the infinite, everlasting, almighty God of this vast universe as revealed to us gradually, step by step, by the demonstrable truths of our savior, science.[6]

Life after Death?

Finally, Edison, like Henry Ford, had a peculiar notion of reincarnation and eternal life which he also associated with his "swarms" of "life entities."

> Now, I shall express another thought which may seem startling. I believe these swarms, or, at least, the individuals which make up these swarms, live forever. Individuals among the entities which form them may change their habitat, leaving one swarm and joining another, so to speak, building corn, for instance, to-day and chickens to-morrow, in accordance with the material which they find at hand to work with.
>
> Frankly, I do not accept the present theories about life and death. I believe, rightly or wrongly, that life is indestructible, it is true, and I also believe that there has always been a fixed quantity of life in this planet, and that this fixed quantity can neither be increased nor decreased. What I believe is that our bodies are made up of myriads of units of life. Our body is not itself the unit of life. It is the tiny entities which may be the cells that are the units of life. We have myriads of cells, and it is the inhabitants in these cells, inhabitants which themselves are beyond the limits of the microscope, which vitalize and "run" our body. To put it in another way, I believe these life-units of which I have spoken band themselves together in countless millions and billions in order to make a man. We have too facilely assumed that the horse or dog is each a unit of life. This, I am convinced, is wrong thinking. The fact is that these "life-units" are too tiny to be seen even by the most high-powered microscope, and so we have assumed that the unit is the man which we can see, and have ignored the existence of the real life-units, which are those we cannot see.[7]

Elementary Particles

As we have seen, Edison fully embraced the theory that all dead and living matter was made up of atoms and molecules, but because he was best acquainted with the laws of electricity, he readily accepted the concept of the electron, which was demonstrated by the English scientist Joseph Thomson in 1897, and therefore it is not surprising that he believed that electrons made up the fundamental life units. He said: "I have had calculations made, and the theory of the electron is, in my view, satisfactory, and makes it quite possible to have a highly organized and developed entity like the human body made up of myriads of electrons, themselves invisible."[8]

The belief in immortality was not just another of his quirks or an expression of the need for a new religious creed. For Edison, it was based on sound observations of the real world. Obviously, it stemmed from the concept of the conservation of energy originally proposed by the English beer brewer and physicist James Joule and later expounded by such men as Herman von Helmholtz and further by the Austrian physicist Ernst Mach, whose theories of units and "things" also encompassed the metaphysical world of the human being and soul. Mach's teachings were translated into English and published in Chicago in 1910.[9]

Immortality

For Edison the question of immortality was related to the survival of life units and new life, which starts with a proper assembly of these basic units that possess the memory of the complete organism: "Everything that pertains to life is still living, and cannot be destroyed." In 1922 many questions remained about the concept of life and immortality according to Edison: "But are all these life-units, or entities, possessed of the same memory, or are some, so to speak, the builders' labourers, and are others the units which direct those labourers? It may be that the great mass of them are workers and a tiny minority directors of the work. That is not a matter about which we can speak with any certainty."[10]

Henry Ford, with his Emersonian optimism and Bible-belt beliefs, did not share the atheist leanings of his mentor but rejoiced when he heard of his interest in life entities and a life hereafter and remarked appreciatively: "The greatest thing that has occurred in the last fifty years is Mr. Edison's conclusion that there is a future life for all of us."[11]

Once Thomas Edison told the Associated Press that in regard to the great beyond and life after death he was "seeking after the truth and had made much progress." Was Edison serious when he released a statement that he was working on a sophisticated and revolutionary new invention, a machine that could trace and measure the energy of the life units? Or was it a trick he liked to play in front of eagerly listening reporters?[12]

The More Einstein the Better

Edison lived in an exciting time of new discoveries that changed the world. He himself had been at the forefront of these developments, and with his burning desire and never-ceasing energy to find explanations to everything, including the mysteries of life and death, he eagerly tried to adopt the teachings of Rudolf Virchow, Louis Pasteur, and Paul Broca in biology and later those of Albert Einstein in physics. Virchow had introduced the concept of cellular pathology, tracing every disease to the basic entity of the cell. Pasteur was the pioneer in microbiology and bacteria, and Broca had charted the brain centers responsible for speech. In 1910 Willem De Vries and Edmund Wilson had demonstrated the importance of chromosomes for cell division.[13]

In later years Edison was particularly impressed by the new teachings of atomic theory, which offered a unified view of all physical matter and energy. He also became familiar with the concept of elementary particles and Einstein's quantum theory and the revolutionary concept of relativity. Edison was not afraid of change. On the contrary, he eagerly followed developments in modern science, and when he was seventy-three he wrote:

> We have been accepting old-established theories with a complacency unworthy even of our present imperfect mental grasp. We need fresh brain-energy among our scientists, new bravery, new initiative. Einstein has shown the world the sort of thought it needs, and it needs it along many lines. The more Einsteins we can get the better. I wish we had an Einstein in every branch of science.
>
> Many great discoveries remain to be made. We must start anew in many things, rejecting the old theories as Einstein did, building along new lines as Einstein did, fearing nothing more than Einstein did.[14]

Edison admitted that he could not understand these intricate concepts based on mathematical deduction. But he had a strong feeling that this young man had something important to say and was sure that he was on the right track. Edison felt connected with this hardworking scientist who once said: "I have little patience with scientists who take a board of wood, look for its thinnest part, and drill a great number of holes where drilling is easy."[15] Was not this exactly the way Edison had worked all his life?

Edison's Religion

In 1890, when Edison was asked if he believed in God, he answered: "Oh, yes; I think all scientific men do that. Or, rather, they don't believe it, they know it. It is for the masses to believe. The scientist knows. When he gets down to earth, though, to a doctrine of atonement, and plan of salvation, and questions of ritual, I'm not in it. I don't go to church much. You see I'm deaf, and can't hear the sermon. And that's the best kind of excuse."[16]

His Bible was the open face of nature, the broad skies, the green plants. In a letter he once said: "I believe in a Supreme Intelligence pervading the Universe."[17]

Edison was a great reader of all kinds of literature from scientific physical, biological, and psychological studies to fiction. In philosophical matters no doubt he had learned from such men as Tom Paine and his *Common Sense* and from Emerson's writings. There are parallels to Emerson in Edison's theory of macro- and microcosm: "The great globe we live on is reproduced in miniature, down to the tiniest detail, in a drop of dew."[18]

The influence of Emerson is evident not only in his theory of microcosm but also in his general approach to life. Edison shared the contemporary optimistic American belief in technical and moral progress through inventions and education, but he did not share the spiritual aspects of transcendentalism. To him religious theories were an excuse for insufficient knowledge, offering a temporary and unsatisfactory solution.

But he agreed with Emerson, who professed: "Why should we grope among dry bones of the past. . . . Undoubtedly we have no questions to ask which are unanswerable. Nature is already in its form and tendencies, describing its own design. Let us interrogate the great apparition that shines so peacefully around us. Let us inquire, to what end is nature?" But in his own realistic way, Edison subscribed to certain transcendental tenets, believing in the unity of man and nature and the supremacy of reason.[19]

Edison saw no need for a religious creed to fill in the unknown, the mysterious. Modern progress in technology and science offered everything and a better life on earth with no need for an unfathomable heaven. Gone were the days of creation, spirits, and humors; now everything could be explained on the basis of tangible elementary units that were responsible for life and disease. Edison fully subscribed to the idea that the answer to the mystery of life and spiritual questions could be found in nature and nowhere else. But in 1930 he confided to a friend: "When you see everything that happens in the world of science and in the working of the universe, you cannot deny that there is a 'Captain on the bridge.'"[20]

Edison had much in common with the naturalist John Burroughs and with Burbank except that he believed that behind all intricate processes of nature there was a creator. Did this mean that he finally surrendered to theistic faith and admitted his failure to find answers through science? It all depends what he meant by "Captain," whether it was God or merely the organization of life units. Perhaps he agreed with Einstein that "God does not play dice."

Electricity Is the Soul of Matter

The naturalist John Burroughs was fascinated by the supreme forces of electricity and admired the electromagnetic world of the wizard: "All matter is charged with electricity, either actual or potential; the sun is hot with it, and doubtless our own heart-beats, our own thinking brains, are intimately related to it; yet it is palpable and visible only in the sudden and extraordinary way. It defies our analysis, it defies our definitions; it is inscrutable and incomprehensible, yet it will do our errands, light our houses, cook our dinners, and pull our loads. . . . Electricity is the soul of the matter."[21]

Edison's faith was similar in many ways to that of John Burroughs, who exclaimed: "The demand of our day is for a scientific religion. This is not a religion in the old ecclesiastical sense, but in the new scientific sense; a religion that moves us to fight vice, crime, war, intemperance, for self-preservation and in brotherly love, and not in obedience to theological dogma or the commands of a God; a religion that opens our eyes to the wonder and beauty of the world. The old religion is a tree that has borne its fruit."[22]

Edison was convinced that many aspects of religious belief are the result of imperfect knowledge and false conceptions of the world in which we live. Both men were confident that science opened a secure road to the future, an optimistic belief in development by reason. Both were Darwinists in the sense that they believed in evolution and the struggle and survival of the fittest. Burroughs said, "Organic evolution upon the earth shows steady and regular progression; as much as the growth of a tree. Chance would have kept things at a standstill. Chance is a man lost in the woods; he never arrives, he wanders aimlessly."[23] Evolution meant betterment of people. So they reasoned after World War I was won, eliminating the evil forces of "Huns." Why fight? A peaceful, easy life could be expected in the foreseeable future enlightened by education and technical progress.

What happended to these optimistic views seventy years ago, after two world wars? Edison and Burroughs certainly did not subscribe to the writings of Oswald Spengler (*Decline of the West*, 1918–22), who greatly influenced pessimistic postwar philosophy. Spengler was of the opinion that history is cyclical rather than progressive and claimed that Western culture had passed its period of creativity and progress and was on the way to destruction.

He was like an inventive obstetrician who, once the baby is delivered, wants to get on to the next pregnancy.

ROBERT CONOT

→12← The Medicine Man

In Edison's time, before the rational development of potent drugs such as antibiotics, medicine was relatively powerless. Doctors may have been adept at physical diagnosis, spotting a disease, or at prognosis, guessing what might happen to the patient with a certain ailment, but they offered little effective treatment. Edison, however, translated his concepts of technology to his own view on diagnostic and therapeutic medicine. Therefore, it is not surprising that he was a pioneer working with X rays, and he also dabbled in patent medicines and had his own theory about the transmission of yellow fever.[1]

With great interest in anything new, he followed the latest developments in medicine and was much impressed by such men as the anthropologist and neurologist Paul Broca and the pioneer of microbiology, Louis Pasteur, whom he visited in Paris in 1889. Pasteur invited him to his new institute, and they "had quite a chat." He watched the inoculation of several persons and studied the treatment with its discoverer as his mentor.[2] While in Europe, he also visited the laboratory in Berlin of the German physiologist Herman von Helmholtz, whom he much admired. He became fascinated by Helmholtz's theory of the conservation of energy and his research on the inner ear and the process of hearing. Later he followed the work of Alexis Carrel, the French-American surgeon and scientist. When in the early 1920s he was asked what he considered the greatest achievement in medicine, he answered "insulin."

Edison's interest in medicine was most evident in his attitude toward his own ailments. Particularly in later years, when his health was failing, he had distinct opinions about his diet and remedies for any disease. He predicted: "The doctor of the future will give no medicine, but will interest his patients in the care of the human frame, in diet and in the cause and prevention of diseases."[3]

Electric Therapy

Edison even meddled in therapeutics and recommended high-voltage electrical shock treatment as a cure for rheumatism, sciatica, gout, and nervous tension. For this procedure he used his own "inductorum," a Ruhmkorff induction coil that transformed the current from a battery into high voltage.[4] As a boy Edison had a reputation for being a healer and earned extra money by administering "electric treatment" using the electrodes of an early telegraph battery. Byron Vanderbilt describes an occasion when a young girl in Port Huron fell on the ice, lost consciousness, and could not be revived. Her physician called young Edison to bring his battery to the sickbed. On directions from the doctor, Edison and his cousin each grasped an electrode and with their free hands massaged the girl's body. After some time, when Edison was gently stroking the girl's forehead, she opened her eyes and came back to consciousness.[5]

Edison already suspected what we know today: brain function and therefore the process of thinking is based on electrical phenomena. He once tried to prove his theory by a crude and unsuccessful experiment. If thinking depended on minute electrical currents generated by the brain, should it not be possible to pick them up and transfer them to his collaborator Charles Batchelor? He fitted electrical induction coils around his and Batchelor's heads and connected them by a wire. Then they sat and thought. At intervals they checked with each other. When they believed that a connection had been established, they found out that it was only the result of a strained imagination.[6]

Edison was a pioneer in his ideas of how drugs should be administered. In 1890 he published "An Account of Some Experiments upon the Application of Electrical Endosmose to the Treatment of Gout." This paper illustrates Edison's genius in tackling a problem physicians had failed to solve. It concerned the therapy for gouty arthritis, which had been attempted by oral administration of lithium salts. The results were not satisfactory because—as Edison reasoned—the therapeutic agent did not reach the inflamed area in sufficiently high concentrations. By applying the laws of electricity and chemistry to medicine, he introduced the modern principle of iontophoresis. When a solution of the negatively charged lithium salt was applied to the skin, the ions would be forced to penetrate the skin by connecting a positive electrode of an electric circuit to the lesion.[7]

Drugs

Edison also had firm opinions about pharmaceuticals. During the stressful years when he was developing the lamp, he had suffered from facial neuralgia, probably a stress headache, caused by holding his head for hours over lamp filaments and models on a workbench. He tried a great variety of pills but finally decided that he would develop his own medicine. In 1878 he came up with the formula for polyform liniment, which contained chloroform, ether, chloral hydrate, peppermint oil, and morphine, for external use. He was satisfied with the result on his own body and two years later registered a patent for the composition, which was produced and sold by the Menlo Park Manufacturing Corporation. Carrying the name of Edison made it an attractive patent medicine, and it was sold until 1950, when morphine was eliminated from the ingredients.

As a cure for gout, Edison suggested use of tetra-ethyl ammonium. The story of its discovery is told as follows:

Edison met a friend one day and, on hearing that he was a great sufferer and noting the swellings of his finger joints, asked with his usual curiosity:

"What is the matter?"

"Gout," replied the sufferer.

"Well, but what is gout?" persisted Edison.

"Deposits of uric acid in the joints," came the reply.

"Why don't the doctors cure you?" asked Edison.

"Because uric acid is insoluble," he was told.

"I don't believe it," said Edison, and went straight to his laboratory, got out many glass tumblers, and into them emptied some of every chemical he possessed. Into each he put a few drops of uric acid and awaited the results. A check forty-eight hours later disclosed that the uric acid had been dissolved in two of the chemicals. One of them was tetra-ethyl ammonium.[8] Therefore, he recommended that compound as a therapeutic agent.

X-Ray Pioneer

In November 1895 Wilhelm Röntgen in Würzburg made a strange discovery: each time he passed a high-voltage electric current through a vacuum tube in a dark room, he observed a faint light shining from a nearby screen. The tube itself did not shine but obviously emitted strange rays that induced fluorescence. Röntgen was captivated by his discovery and became convinced of its importance when he saw that the radiation applied to his wife's hand left a picture of her bone on a photographic plate. On December 28, 1895, Röntgen reported that he had discovered a mysterious radiation that could penetrate soft tissues of the body and blacken photographic plates. News of the discovery spread rapidly all over the world. On January 6, 1896, it was publicized by the *New York Sun*.

Edison was fascinated by this report and urged his collaborators to drop everything and start experiments on radiation. He said: "We could do a lot of things before others get their second wind." The method of producing these mysterious rays was familiar to him because it closely followed his own line of research when working on light bulbs, inducing the "Edison effect," the passage of electricity from a filament to a plate inside a glass tube. The X-ray tube is similar in that a filament heated by electric current emits electrons that strike a metal plate and cause emission of a penetrating radiation of short wavelength.

Five days later he started experimenting with the new radiation, making his own X-ray tubes. Soon he was able to confirm Röntgen's findings: the rays were invisible to the naked eye but left an imprint on a photographic plate. When the rays were directed to his assistant's hand, they penetrated the skin and muscles but left an imprint of white skeletal shadows of the bones. Edison immediately realized the immense potential of X rays in medicine for diagnostic purposes.[9]

The original demonstration of X rays had been done by exposure on a photographic plate, but Edison wanted fast visualization. Being an expert in chemistry, he tested a large number of compounds (upward of eight thousand) and finally found out that calcium tungstate when struck by X rays would produce a visible picture by fluorescence. He was now able to see bones of the hand directly as an X-ray picture. This discovery led to the development of the fluoroscope, a viewing screen covered with a layer of calcium tungstate, which is now an established piece of equipment in radiology and gave rise to the term *fluoroscopy*. Nicholas Pupin at Columbia University in New York made use of Edison's invention to perform radiographs using this intensifying screen.

The first piece of equipment Edison put on the market in 1896 was called a vitascope, a little peephole fluoroscope for medical and personal use.

Edison was soon recognized as an expert in the field of X rays and received many requests for help from physicians. The most spectacular such request came in September 1901, when President William McKinley was shot at the Pan-American Exposition in Buffalo. The Edison laboratory received a telephone message asking if an X-ray machine could be sent immediately to enable physicians to locate the bullet. Edison dispatched the equipment together with his young technician Clarence Dally, who arrived in Buffalo the following morning. Dally was busy installing the machine when he received a message saying that an investigation would not be required for at least a week because the president's condition had improved and it was considered unwise to search for the bullet just then. The doctors had concluded that the missile was lodged in a spot where it might safely remain without endangering the president's chance of recovery. One of the bullets had penetrated the abdomen and probably lodged in his back. Dally decided to leave Buffalo. He wanted to see Niagara Falls before returning to New York. A few days later, McKinley's condition took a sudden and alarming change for the worse. Finally the president died. It was expected that the bullet would be found during the autopsy. But when it could not be detected, a new call went out for an X ray. But Edison's machine was not used. This event illustrates how little knowledge the supposedly best physicians of the time had. They did not understand the usefulness of a simple X-ray picture.

While working with X rays, Edison soon learned about the hazards of this new type of radiation. He complained of abdominal cramps and defective vision, which disappeared after some time, but Clarence Dally, who had produced thousands of X-ray tubes and tested each personally by placing his hand directly under the beam, started to develop skin burns followed by ulceration. Edison remarked: "I started to make a number of these lamps, but soon found that the X-rays had affected poisonously my assistant, Mr. Dally, so that his hair came out and his flesh commenced to ulcerate. I then concluded that it would not do, and that it would not be a very popular kind of light, so I dropped it." That decision came too late for Dally, who died in 1904 of metastatic carcinoma after both arms had been amputated.[10]

Edison—like Röntgen—never obtained a patent for his invention, and he donated X-ray tubes to various hospitals.

Flying Syringes

Edison was obsessed by elementary particles, which he considered the foundation of all living and dead matter. Therefore, he was also interested in microorganisms such as bacteria, and particularly after his visit in 1889 to Louis Pasteur in Paris he became fascinated by the life that could be exposed under the microscope. At the time the focus was on deadly microbes rather than on the concept of the useful role of an animal-bacteria relationship, which Pasteur also predicted.

The early twentieth century was an era of great accomplishments in bacteriology and immunology. Scientists realized that microbial infections were caused by poisonous substances, toxins, produced by bacteria. The concept of exotoxins excreted by live bacteria or endotoxins liberated from dying bugs was introduced. Focal infections were found to be responsible for a variety of ailments such as rheumatic fever and many aches and pains. Infected dental roots and smoldering infections in the colon were targeted for treatment. Teeth had to be extracted and a diet regimen introduced that did not give nasty bugs a chance of multiplying in the gut. When Edison complained about pain in his leg, his physician suggested an X ray to find out if there were undrained pockets in his jaws, but he declined and decided to have all his teeth pulled.[11] From previous bad experience when working with the vitascope he was afraid of exposure to the deadly radiation. He tried to check infection of the colon with strange diets and periods of fasting.[12]

At the turn of the century in Florida yellow fever was a real threat. It was raging in South America and nearby Cuba, and there had been outbreaks in Florida as well. Before U.S. Army physician Walter Reed presented conclusive evidence that the disease was caused by tiny living matter and transmitted by mosquitoes that acted like "flying syringes," Edison came up with the idea that "the fever microbe is parasitic, as it travels slowly along the ground and is known to have been stopped in some cases by the repaving of streets." He thought that the fever germs could be transmitted by ants, clams, and earthworms, and he reasoned that "the only way to stop the spread of disease is to put a cordon of gasoline around the infected place."[13] He also developed his own pesticide, a mixture of caustic soda and rhigolene.

The Human Stomach

Edison had decided opinions about what people should eat. He said, "Food should be to the body what coal is to the boiler of a steam engine. We are nothing but machinery, meat machinery." But the "coal" should be of the best quality. He believed in a healthy lifestyle, particularly in diet. He did not believe in physical exercise of the body but was convinced that training of the brain was a necessity; otherwise "the brain will atrophy."

He firmly believed that half of all illnesses were caused by excessive eating. Once he said to a friend with heart trouble: "Americans dig their grave with their teeth. Nearly all of our ailments and distempers come by way of mouth. Your heart will be alright if you let up on eating and spend one third of your time collecting funny stories." He echoed his friend John Burroughs, who said: "Man's stomach is the battle ground of his life." "In the case of animals the taste or appetite is a safe guide. What the creature loves, that agrees with it, or *vice versa*." "With man his appetite is not a safe guide."[14]

Edison was suspicious of all uncooked food because it might carry typhoid bacteria, and he was terrified that there might be nasty bugs in his colon. In 1924 he launched an attack on "the travelling poison factory" of his lower bowel. He wanted to starve the bacilli to death and "not make toxins to poison the whole system."[15]

Edison experimented with different diets and found out that his gastric pain (most probably from an ulcer) could be relieved by drinking milk. He insisted on drinking a pint of milk every two to three hours. Thus he had to be sure that the milk came from a reliable source and at times kept his own cows in Fort Myers, just as he did up north at his Glenmont estate.

Edison characteristically remarked: "We resort to all sorts of artificial and harmful stimulants."[16] He disliked alcoholic beverages and in 1922 said, "Every man with brains ought to take a pledge to vote to make liquor impossible." He hated cigarettes (because they burned paper), although he smoked big cigars and chewed tobacco.

His best friend, Henry Ford, also was very interested in health care, medical treatment, and diet. He had innovative ideas about hospital care. In 1914 he built a "human garage" in Detroit, which he considered "the best hospital in the world," to care for his workers at fixed prices and pay doctors fixed salaries, a new concept at the time. "It is my shop," Ford said, "where I hope people can get well as rapidly as possible and have their injured parts repaired." But he also had bizarre ideas about medicine and food: "If people would learn to eat the things they should, there would be no need for hospitals. Jails and prisons would have less to do." "Pay no attention to that doctor," he said to a patient with heart trouble. "All you have to do is get out of bed and lie on the floor for half an hour twice a day and eat celery and carrots: then you'll be all right."[17]

Engraved Speech

To Edison, the most important use of the phonograph was not for entertainment but for dictation, "reading to inmates of blind asylums, to teach children the alphabet," and to teach languages: "Suppose Stanley had had one and thus obtained for the world all the dialects of Central Africa. It will be used to make toys talk." He also expected that the phonograph would open up new medical possibilities, and he predicted the introduction of phonocardiography (recording of cardiac sounds and murmurs): "Who can fail to make the nice distinctions between every form of bronchial and pulmonary rale, percussion, succussion and friction sounds, surgical crepitus, fetal and placental murmurs and arterial and cardiac bruit, when each can be produced at will, amplified to any desired extent, in the study, the amphitheatre, the office, the hospital? The lecturer of the future will teach more effectively with this instrument than by the mouth."[18]

The phonograph was Edison's favorite invention in part because of his hearing problem. He was impressed by "visible speech" that he could see in the phonograph foil when amplified by a microscope, and he wanted to test the hypothesis that indentations could be read with the eye: "Microscopic examination of the indentations made in tin foil by the phonograph when spoken to, shows that each letter has a definitive form, though there is great variation, resulting from the intensity and difference of voice. Long E (or ay) on the foil looks like two indian clubs with the handles together."[19]

He Lives in a World Apart

Edison was not stone deaf, but he was hard of hearing from the time he was a young boy. His deafness has been ascribed to a blow to his head which he received as a punishment from a "dour Scot by the name of Alexander Stevenson" when his boyhood laboratory in the baggage car of a train erupted in flames. Even Edison believed in that traumatic cause of his deafness, which he described: "The blow at this time by Stevenson may have started it, but it was finished one day when I was standing on the station platform at Smith's Creek. I was trying to climb into the freight car with both arms full of papers when the conductor, attempting to help me, took me by the ears and lifted me up into the train. I felt something snap inside my head and my deafness started from that time and has ever since progressed."[20]

A much more likely cause of Edison's hearing loss was his chronic ear infections. He was a sickly boy and from early childhood was prone to infections such as bronchitis.[21] In the winter months his ears often became inflamed. When he was seven years old, he had scarlatina (scarlet fever), a streptococcal infection that can affect the ear.[22] These frequent illnesses caused him to miss so much school that his mother had him privately tutored at home. Even in adulthood Edison suffered from repeated upper respiratory infections such as in 1884–85 and 1887. These infections were probably also associated with ear infections, although there is no direct evidence that they were.

Ear infection—otitis media—with accumulation of fluid in the middle ear is the most common cause of temporary and sometimes permanent hearing loss in children and adults. It is usually the result of bacterial infection as a complication of upper respiratory infections, influenza, scarlet fever, or measles. Before the introduction of antibiotics, the condition often became chronic and the inflammatory process would extend to the mastoid bones. In fact, Edison was operated on for mastoiditis in 1887, in 1905, and in 1908.[23] Repeated ear infections damage the middle ear, which contains the organs that transmit the sound vibrations to the sensory organ in the inner ear. (The middle ear begins with the eardrum, which contains the ossicles, three delicate bones linked to the inner ear. Sound vibrations are transmitted by the lever system of the ossicles to the sound-sensing organ of the inner ear, or cochlea.)

The inner ear with the sensory organ for hearing was not affected because Edison could perceive sound by bone conduction of vibrations through the cranium, bypassing the middle ear. Therefore, he could hear music from a piano or his own invention, the phonograph, if he bit the wooden frame of the instrument. He also developed an amazing ability to read lips so that he could "listen" to others far beyond the distance normal persons can hear. Communication was sometimes supplemented when Mina tapped messages on his knee using the Morse code. In fact, that is how they communicated early on and was the way he proposed to her.

Edison's oldest son from his second marriage, Charles, also had a hearing problem. He recalled in his taped memoirs: "The reason I didn't get into the war in active service was my deafness. It worried me a great deal that I was not carrying a gun or sailing on a ship." Charles, like his father, became increasingly deaf as he grew older. He thought it stemmed from typhoid fever, but that is very unlikely. When he was eighteen, he had an operation for mastoiditis.[24]

Might deafness in the Edison family have been a genetic disorder such as otosclerosis? Today this disease is the most common cause of conductive hearing loss in people between the ages of fifteen and fifty years. It is a defect that causes the inner ear capsule to be overgrown by abnormal bone. The process causes increasing fixation of the footplate of the stapes, which is responsible for transmitting vibrations to the sensory organ of the inner ear. This abnormality causes progressive conduction hearing impairment. Hearing loss is usually first noticed when the person is in the late teens or early twenties. Both ears are usually affected, but not always. There is a family history of the problem in 50 percent of cases, and it occurs in about the same incidence in males and females (although pregnancy may accelerate the condition). Fair-complexioned persons are more prone to the disease than those who are dark-skinned. Ear infections may accelerate the hearing loss in otosclerosis.[25] That the Edisons had a genetic disposition for the condition cannot be ruled out.

Edison was never much worried about his hearing problem. In fact, he thought it was an advantage because it shielded him from distracting noise and talk and thus was a blessing in disguise that allowed him to concentrate on activities he enjoyed. Edison thought his deafness contributed to the development of the telephone and phonograph. Mina Edison said: "He does not consider his deafness an affliction. He says it has contributed greatly to his powers of concentration, and has allowed him to seek within himself for his amusements. He really lives in a world apart."[26]

Edison became so accustomed to his disability that he considered restoration of hearing an affliction rather than a benefit. If deafness was not a problem in conversation—he could read lips, he communicated with Mina by tapping the Morse code—it must have been a handicap when listening to music. When asked what he thought was his greatest invention, he answered: "I like the phonograph best. Doubtless this is because I love music."[27]

How could Edison enjoy music and be critical about music, particularly when testing his own phonographs and the large number of records made in his studios in New York? He had tricks that enabled him to hear by bone conduction, particularly the high notes. He had his special way of listening: "He checked everything by using a medium-sized horn from one of his old phonographs to the small end of which he attached a piece of rubber which fitted closely over his good ear. The other end he would place in the end of the horn of one of his largest phonographs. Sometimes he would listen by placing a pencil between his teeth and resting the other end against the phonograph case. Or he would bite the wood, seeking in this way to get the vibrations of the music through the bones of his head."[28]

Henry Ford was always concerned about his friend and neighbor at Fort Myers and once presented him with new hearing aids. Mrs. Edison tried to attract her husband's attention, saying:

"Mr. Ford has brought some hearing aids for you, Dearie—three of the best in the world."

Edison smiled and said, "No thanks."

"Why?" Ford asked.

"Well, if one of them worked, I'd have to listen to what you folks are saying, instead of getting along with my reading." Then he added: "If one of them worked, Mina would make me go to church with her every Sunday."

Nobody would accept this reasoning, but he came up with several more lame excuses. Then he admitted that when he was a young man running the Menlo Park plant, someone had convinced him to use an ear trumpet, a primitive hearing aid. As he walked into the plant one day, a crisis was brewing, and the superintendent, a big Irishman who had been used to shouting at Edison for years, grabbed the ear trumpet and yelled into it. It nearly took the top off Edison's head. He threw the instrument down and would have nothing to do with hearing aids from then on.[29]

Another great inventor who benefited from deafness was Alexander Graham Bell. He had no hearing problems himself but was stimulated in his research on reproduction of sound because of the deafness of his wife, Mabel. Bell experimented with visible models of speech and electrical transmission of sound in his telephone. He wanted to "make a current of electricity vary in intensity precisely as the air waves in density during the production of sound." He managed to do this when he let sound waves vibrate a membrane, which induced an electric current that could make another receiver-membrane do the same at the other end. Edison also worked with the telephone and greatly perfected its performance to make it commercially available.

It is a coincidence that Juan Ponce de Leon, the discoverer of Florida, was a close relative of the pioneer in educating the deaf, the Spanish Benedictine monk Pedro Ponce de Leon. Born in about 1520 at Valladolid, Ponce de Leon taught speech by articulation. His interest in the deaf started when he allowed a young deaf-mute boy, Gaspard Burgos, to enter the monastery as a novice after Ponce de Leon taught him to write and speak so that he could confess his sins.

According to Spanish law, deaf and dumb persons were legally incapable and could not inherit estate or title. It was therefore a great achievement of Ponce de Leon that he was able to help sons of influential families with this handicap to communicate by speech. After the death of Ponce de Leon, his pioneering work was carried on by his successors, and in 1620 the first treatise on the education of the deaf was published. It contained analogies of letters of the alphabet with their phonetic counterparts and thus can be claimed as the forerunner of Bell's "visible speech."[30]

Edison never admitted that his deafness was a handicap. Despite many failures in his work, sickness, and a big fire that destroyed most of his West Orange laboratory, he always was optimistic and saw the bright side in life. When talking about movies, he once said: "It's astounding how much more a deaf person can see."

I would not leave anything to a man of action,
as he would be tempted to give up work.
On the other hand I would like to help dreamers,
as they find it difficult to get on in life.

ALFRED NOBEL, 1884

→ 13 ← The Nobel Prize

Alfred Nobel, the Swedish scientist and inventor, was a pioneer in the manufacture of explosives and weapons and in oil exploration; he also was a man
of vision. Nobel was a paradox, a pacifist at heart who invented dynamite
and an immensely successful businessman embarrassed by his riches, who
at his death, childless, in 1896 left a large fortune. He was deeply interested
in world peace and the improvement of living conditions of mankind. He
chose to give his estate to create a fund that could be used to award prizes to
persons who had rendered great service in science and peaceful human re-
lations. He specified that "the prizes should be distributed without regard to
nationality, so that the prize may be awarded in all cases to the most deserv-
ing, be he Scandinavian or not."[1]

Edison and the Nobel Prize

Undoubtedly Edison was highly qualified for the Nobel Prize in physics.
There is no question that his inventions and applied science rendered great
services to mankind. He was a man of vision whose work helped shape the

future. Even though he always stressed the practicality of his inventions and was indifferent to the work of "eggheads," theoretical scientists, his contributions had enormous implications for the development of theories and concepts in physics. The two-electrode bulb of 1883, which exhibited the "Edison effect" or thermionic emission, was the forerunner of the vacuum tube, the basis of electronic amplification. Therefore, Edison may justly be regarded as the "father of modern electronics."[2]

Why was Edison never selected by the Nobel Committee to receive the coveted prize? Few people know that Thomas Alva Edison was on the short list for the 1915 Nobel Prize in physics at a time when all his major achievements had been accomplished. He was proposed by an external member of the Swedish Royal Academy of Sciences, Henry Fairfield Osborn, professor at Columbia University and director of the Museum of Natural History in New York City.[3]

It is not surprising that his name was presented to the Royal Academy of Sciences in Stockholm because of the immense impact his inventions had on the development of physical sciences. In the past the academy had been much impressed by the pioneers of electricity, and until 1915 four prizes had been awarded to persons whose discoveries were connected with electromagnetism and X rays, but the real pioneer in this field, Edison, had always been bypassed. Now, many members of the Swedish Royal Academy of Sciences no doubt thought it was time to honor the old man, but in the end he was rejected because he did not belong to the establishment of academic scientists such as Wilhelm Conrad Röntgen, who in 1901 received the first prize for his discovery of the X ray, or later Henri Becquerel and Marie Curie. Until 1915 all recipients had been university professors of physics. This tradition was broken only in 1912, when the prize was offered to Nils Gustaf Dalén, a Swedish engineer.[4]

Reputedly, the academy considered giving a joint award to Nicola Tesla and Edison. According to R. W. Clark, the 1912 prize was offered to Tesla for his inventions in transmission of high-voltage electricity. The prize was to be awarded with the provision that it be shared with Edison. Because of an old animosity against Edison, it was said that Tesla declined and the prize instead went to Nils Gustaf Dalén "for his discovery of automatic regulators, which can be used in conjunction with gas accumulators for lighthouses and lightships."[5]

In reality, neither Tesla nor Edison was on the short list for the 1912 Nobel Prize in physics, and the rumor that Tesla refused to receive the prize together with Edison is fiction because the award procedure is such that potential candidates are never notified before the final choice of the Swedish Royal Academy of Sciences is made public each year in October.

In 1915 rumors again connected Tesla with the coveted prize. The *New York Times* on November 6 reported that Tesla and Edison were to share the Nobel Prize in physics. The following day in an interview Tesla stated that he had not received official notification, but he speculated that he was to receive the award for his discovery of a way to transmit electric waves through the air. Tesla, with inflated self-confidence, was convinced that he deserved the prize for dozens of his creations: "For any of these I would give all the Nobel prizes during the next thousand years."

Edison was informed of the rumor that he was to receive the award when he was on his way back from the Panama Pacific Exposition in San Francisco. He was much more realistic about the prospect of being selected for such a great honor. He seemed surprised and confirmed that he had not been notified either.

The initial press report sparked a succession of enthusiastic articles in daily papers and magazines, including the *Literary Digest* and *Electrical World*.[6] By this time, a Reuters cable from London finally put an end to the speculations: the Nobel Committee in Stockholm announced that the prize for 1915 was awarded to Professor W. H. Bragg of London University and his son W. L. Bragg, professor at the Victoria University of Manchester, "for their services in the investigation of the structure of crystals, by means of Röntgen rays."[7]

In 1937 Tesla was nominated for his research in high-frequency currents and electromagnetism. The Austrian Academy of Sciences had been so impressed by his achievements that it nominated him for the award at the 1936 Tesla Festival in Belgrade, stating that "for his immortal discoveries" he should be honored with the Nobel Prize in physics.[8] Ultimately, however, neither Edison nor Tesla was awarded the Nobel Prize.

Tesla was an eccentric genius whose pioneering work on alternating currents made an important contribution to physics. At the turn of the century Tesla had been a rising star in both the United States and Europe. Once when he lectured in London to the Royal Society, his hosts were so impressed that they escorted him to Michael Faraday's chair and gave him a generous portion of the great scientist's own whiskey to drink.[9]

In 1882 Edison hired Tesla to make improvements in electric motors and power generators. Tesla not only possessed an imaginative mind but proved to be a successful engineer in Edison's laboratory. The collaboration, however, did not last very long because of personal differences. In the end he squabbled with Edison over a salary raise Edison had jokingly promised for improvements on a dynamo (Tesla asked for $50,000). When questioned, Edison answered: "Tesla, you don't understand American humor." Tesla left, enraged, to pursue his own career, which laid the ground for the development of alternating current.[10]

Tesla and Edison were extremely different in all ways. Tesla had a university education and was an abstract thinker. He preferred theoretical deduction rather than Edison's use of trial and error. Tesla later ridiculed his master when he said:

> If he had a needle to find in a haystack, he would not stop to reason where it was most likely to be, he would proceed at once with the feverish diligence of the bee to examine straw after straw until he found the object of his search. His method was inefficient in the extreme, for an immense ground had to be covered to get anything at all unless blind chance intervened, and at first I was almost a sorry witness of his doings, knowing that just a little theory and calculation would have saved him 90 per cent of the labor. But he has a veritable contempt for book learning and mathematical knowledge, trusting himself entirely to his inventor's instinct and practical American sense.[11]

Tesla possessed a vivid imagination with flashes of genius and sometimes weird inspirations which he tried to pursue. On the personal level, the two men had completely different outlooks on life: Edison the rugged, humorous, hardworking, unpolished self-made man, Tesla a serious, theoretical, ec-centric dandy.

After working with Edison, Tesla moved to New York, lived in expensive hotels, and established a laboratory in Manhattan which became a meeting place of the rich and famous. He gave spectacular demonstrations and appeared as a magician, elegantly dressed in tails and white tie. He attracted skeptical scientists and capitalists but also artists and poets, including Mark Twain, Rudyard Kipling, and John Muir.

Awards to Edison

Thomas Edison probably never expected to join the ranks of Nobel laureates. Nevertheless, he was richly rewarded with international and national medals and prizes. In 1881 he was made a Companion of the Légion d'honneur, and in 1889, while in Paris, he was promoted to its highest rank. He also received the Cross of Grand Officer in Italy (1889), the Albert Medal of the British Society of Arts (1892), the Rathenau Gold Medal in Germany

(1915), the Medal of the Franklin Institute (1915), and the Congressional Gold Medal (1928).

He was accepted by the academic world, receiving honorary doctorates of philosophy from Union College in Schenectady and in science from Princeton University. He was also given an honorary degree from an academic institution in Florida: Rollins College of Winter Park. As late as 1992, Edison was posthumously awarded a bachelor of science degree by the Thomas Edison College of Trenton, New Jersey. This institution is the first college in the United States devoted solely to granting degrees to people who have knowledge equivalent to that normally offered in a classroom and who want to get credit for degrees by demonstrating their knowledge. At the ceremony the college's president, George R. Pruitt, said the degree was not honorary but was earned by Edison, the self-educated inventor of the light bulb and phonograph. To prove his point, he had received seventeen portfolios detailing the inventor's research from members of the Edison Papers project at Rutgers University. After evaluating the material, the college faculty granted Edison a degree in applied science and technology.[12]

Edison never boasted about his decorations. On the contrary, he always avoided answering questions about the medals with the comment that he had a "couple of quarts" of them up in the house, and after he had received the decoration of the Legion d'honneur in Paris he hid the ribbon because he did not want to show off.[13]

Few individuals can stand the test of fame and emerge from it as simple, kindly and unassuming.

ALLEN H. ANDREWS, DESCRIBING EDISON, 1950

→ 14 ← Gentle Giant?

In Fort Myers Edison fast became the town's greatest publicity agent. Everybody loved him for his kind personality. The residents looked forward to his annual winter visit. The Edisons usually came early in February before Thomas's birthday, February 11, or by their wedding anniversary, the twenty-fourth.

Gentle but Stubborn

The image of Edison as a gentle, friendly giant is not correct. Like many successful great men, he was very self-centered and stubborn. Obviously his deafness also affected his behavior. His dedication to work made him a poor family man. According to Robert Conot, he seldom cultivated friendships but considered his acquaintances dispensable, to be used for his own advantage and advancement. His ethics and standards were his own, and when they conflicted with his drive for success, they could be overridden.[1] Actually, however, he cultivated some social relationships, particularly in Florida, and probably because of the efforts of Mina, who was a tireless correspondent both to friends and family. Edison could be tough when negotiating with partners or giving orders to co-workers. He did not have an egalitarian relationship of give and take of ideas with his co-workers though he considered them buddies.

Edison did not have much time for the three children from his first marriage, whom he neglected. The situation was different for Charles, Madeleine, and Theodore, the children from his second marriage, because Mina not only paid much attention to them but also tried to look after Edison's unlucky first brood. It was not an easy task because Edison considered them the result of a "failed experiment," and Mina often had to intervene on their behalf.

In Florida he was more at ease and less involved in the many pressing obligations of work and could spend more time with his family, friends, and visiting co-workers. The atmosphere of Fort Myers seemed to bring out the positive side of his character. One Fort Myers resident wrote of him:

> It is about the lesser known Edison, the man, fellow citizen and neighbor that we write as he was known by his Lee County friends and admirers,—one who had a pleasant smile and a cheery greeting for all with whom he came in contact. Few individuals can stand the test of fame and emerge from it as simple, kindly and unassuming. For in the average man there is something in the applause of the crowd and the stimulus of publicity that intoxicates and causes him to lose all sense of proportion and to magnify his personal achievements.

The author of these lines, a neighbor, also wrote:

> On Saturday night in 1929, when the nation at large was celebrating the fiftieth anniversary of Edison's invention of the incandescent light Mr. and Mrs. Edison and her brother, Mr. Miller, were eating their supper by candlelight in a little rustic tea garden in Estero where they found refuge from a violent electric storm. It all happened this way: The distinguished party were returning about 8 pm from some point of interest they had visited down the Tamiami Trail and when nearing Estero were overtaken by a storm of violent intensity. Drenched to the skin, they sought refuge in the rustic palm-thatched building of the local tea garden and there found cordial hospitality, dry shelter, warm food and drink. While eating supper the electric lights went out. Candles were brought in, and there in simple and rustic surroundings

amid the booming thunder and vivid flashing of lightning the electrical wizard and his companions finished their evening meal in contentment and awaited the abatement of the storm.[2]

Particularly in Florida, Edison could spend time with his children in leisure activities such as boating, fishing, shelling, and simply being together on the broad verandas of Seminole Lodge. In later years he became very fond of children. Robert C. Halgrim of Fort Myers remembers: "He always found time for a child when often he could not be bothered with an adult. I believe it was because he hoped that he might encourage them through his association with them. I have watched him go out of his way many times to let them take his picture and chat with them, although because of his deafness he had to do most of the talking."[3]

The wife of a former pupil of the Edison High School whom I met in Fort Myers testified that her husband remembered the great man who used to pass by and liked to chat with him and other children. Another story tells of Edison in his late years going out in Fort Myers with pockets full of dimes which he handed out to children he met.

Edison was a man with simple personal tastes and unostentatious behavior. Once, when invited to a public dinner in his honor, he declined, stating: "One hundred thousand dollars would not tempt me to sit through two hours of personal glorification." He disliked notoriety and said: "A man is to be measured by what he does, and not by what is said about him."[4]

Although Edison was involved with the Naval Consulting Board during World War I, the Official Florida Bicentennial Commemorative Book downplays the accomplishments of the great inventor: "America fought three major wars during Thomas Edison's lifetime, yet he made virtually no direct impact on military technology. This is not surprising. A man who placed bird houses on posts offshore in the river to effect a truce between birds and cats is not likely to devote his energies to weapons of destruction." "Making things which kill men is against my fiber," Edison once said. "I would rather make people laugh."[5]

Famous Guests

After 1901, when Edison resumed his yearly visits to Fort Myers, he and Mina became the main attraction of the town and often received famous guests. The Edison home, however, was not the scene of big parties as was the nearby Murphy-Burroughs home. But a guest book and names on the stones of Friendship Walk in the garden of Seminole Lodge bear testimony to the visits of many intellectuals and industry leaders such as Richard Colgate and Friedrich Merck.

One friend of Edison's whose actions had a major impact on Florida was Barron Collier, who in 1921 started creating his one-million-acre empire in southwest Florida and who promised to complete the Tamiami Trail by building the first bridge over the Caloosahatchee near Fort Myers. President-elect Herbert Hoover in February 1929 came from Miami to honor Edison on his birthday. This trip was part of a Miami–Lake Region tour, arranged by Governor Doyle Carlton, who sought federal aid for a flood protection plan in the aftermath of the 1926–28 hurricanes that had disastrous effects for south Florida and especially the Lake Okeechobee area.

Another important visitor at Seminole Lodge was Emil Ludwig, the German writer and biographer of Napoleon. When later asked who was the greatest man he met in America, President Wilson, Paderewski, or Henry Ford, he said: "It is none of them, but Thomas Edison." The interrogator was disappointed. "But why Edison?"

> No, it wasn't the electric lamp or the phonograph. Edison had the kind of overpowering personality that conquered everyone he came in contact with. As an old man, when I saw him, there was something really Olympian about him: his venerable white head that never bowed with age but only grew more stately, his youthful laugh, the high voice characteristic of the hard of hearing, complete naturalness, radiant cheer,—these would be enough if I were to see him sitting there on the sand in the setting sun, without knowing who he was, to attract me magnetically and make me ask, "who is that perfect man?" He looks like God might have imagined him. And then add the realization of his tremendous achievement and his versatility. Our imagination associates this great figure with all the works he conceived, with the struggles in which he overcame his opponents, with the brilliant flashes of thought with which he enlightened the world. You will never find anything like that in Orville Wright, who was also a great inventor, nor Henry Ford, nor Paderewski, nor in Wilson, and they all accomplished great things in our days.[6]

This word portrait describes Edison well. It brings forward an important point, missed by many: "the brilliant flashes of thought," his imagination, which enabled him to achieve his results.

One of Edison's staunchest admirers was Louis Pasteur, a man who was not afflicted with modesty. He said: "Your Edison is a great man. When the history of our generation comes to be written two names that will stand out most prominently in science will be his and mine."[7]

Myths

The early accounts of the inventor that had reached Florida were influenced by the popular misgivings and frightening myths about modern inventions and machines. To the simple Floridian Edison represented a modern Prometheus who had stolen the light from the gods. People in Florida did not know how to approach him or what to say to him, therefore they called him the "great inventor," "Wizard of Electricity," the Ph.D., professor from the North. Later, when the blessings of civilization reached Florida, they admired him as a benefactor of mankind, and the pessimistic twentieth-century questioning of the value of technical progress never fully reached Fort Myers.

In Fort Myers Edison was immensely popular, but from the very beginning his name seemed to be surrounded by an aura of mystery. When the laboratory equipment shipped to Florida was to be unloaded, it was difficult to get hands to take his apparatus from the boats. "They won't touch any of it, for fear, as they say, 'some ob dem infernal machines gwine to bust.'"[8]

The Edison name was liberally used to honor cultural establishments such as the new Edison Park School and to publicize business enterprises such as the Edison National Bank (now Barnett Bank) and the Edison Mall. Downtown in Centennial Park a statue called *Uncommon Friends* by a local sculptor, Don Wilkins, displays the bronze figures of Thomas Edison, Henry Ford, and Harvey Firestone. *Uncommon Friends* also is the title of a book by a good friend of the Edisons, James Newton of Fort Myers Beach.

It is not surprising that during the many years Edison spent in Fort Myers many stories were told about the great man, stories not based on facts but perpetuated over time so that they were taken for granted and became accepted as fact. The best-known story is the 1887 tale of Edison promising to give the townspeople street lighting and even electric streetcars. It is said that Edison offered to provide the town with a system of electric lights at no charge. The town contemplated the gift but rejected it because it would have to provide the poles, which would be expensive, and such lights might keep the cows awake at night and cause havoc in the streets. (Electric lighting came to the town of Fort Myers in 1898 and was installed by an enterprising businessman.)

Another story concerns the visit of the Duke of Sutherland during a fishing trip with the Edisons in Fort Myers. According to Karl A. Bickel, the duke arrived on his large steam yacht, the *Sans Peur*, and tied up at the old city dock at the foot of Jackson Street. Attended by four kilted Scottish pipers "tootling their heads off," the duke came up the palm-lined streets to Seminole Lodge.[9] It is likely that the duke came to Fort Myers to visit the inventor because he had met him before while in New York. But had he truly been accompanied by Scottish pipers, the news-hungry editor of the *Fort Myers Press* surely would have made it a major story.

Another myth concerns bamboo-reinforced concrete used for building Edison's swimming pool in 1910. This was hailed as another great invention that could be used as a substitute for steel wires. Detailed instructions and records kept by the contractor about the construction survive, and they do not mention using bamboo in the concrete.[10]

The myth persists that while at Seminole Lodge Edison's fishing was often symbolic and many times he did not bait his line. He could be seen sitting for hours on the long pier angling, like Rip van Winkle, who fished all day without a murmur, even though he was not encouraged by a single nibble. That story probably is not true because Edison frequently complained of unsuccessful efforts, and Mina had arranged for the river to be stocked with fish. There were also many proud reports about successful fishing activities in Fort Myers such as in 1902 and 1914: "We catch from 2 to 4 sharks a day off dock and tarpon are running in the river east."[11]

Edison's Eden

For the Edison family Fort Myers was a state of mind, a feeling, as much as a location. Edison considered Seminole Lodge the most beautiful spot in the world. It was his Garden of Eden. There was nothing on earth like it, and it was "as near heaven as I want to be." He once wrote: "There are over one hundred million people in the United States, but only one Ft. Myers, the flower city of Tropical Florida."[12]

Fort Myers certainly proved to be a Fountain of Youth for Edison, who started wintering there when he was thirty-five and lived until the age of eighty-four despite many infirmities. In 1926 he said:

Not infrequently I am asked what contribution Florida has made to me. Pleasure, rest and recreation are real but not necessarily tangible assets, but in addition to these things, I feel that at the least Florida has given me five years of additional life. Perhaps I can stretch it out to six or seven years, but of five years I am reasonable certain. I am not over-fond of pneumonia so common in the North. Florida is a great State for old folks, when they haven't the vitality they once had. This has been discovered by a great many people, and to me it affords assurance that Florida will never be forgotten. There are a great many more men and women living in the North who only have to get in the sunshine for one winter to become real enthusiastic for the State, as well as annual visitors.[13]

Until the end of his life, Fort Myers was his favorite place, even when he started having symptoms of old age affecting his memory. In May 1929 Mina wrote from Fort Myers: "There is one thing I notice very much is that he cannot remember so well recent things but past matters he remembers very well. But he is very happy these days and often sits out under the tree and sings. Not hum, but sings out loud."[14]

*The Pageant of Light, a week long gala on
Edison's birthday, has become to Fort Myers
what the Mardi Gras is to New Orleans.*

JOHN D. VENABLE, 1978

⇒ 15 ⇐ The Edison-Ford Winter Estates

After the death of Thomas A. Edison in 1931, Mina with her children and grandchildren continued to come to Seminole Lodge, but the laboratory stood deserted. Everybody missed the great man who had meant so much for Fort Myers and the nation.

Over the years Edison's winter home in Fort Myers has become the most important monument to the great inventor except for the Edison National Historic Site in West Orange, New Jersey, and the Edison laboratories at Greenfield Village, Dearborn, Michigan. The Edison winter home has the advantage of having the most diverse exhibitions on display. They include not only a large collection of technical memorabilia but also living tokens such as plants, trees, and flowers that were part of the life of America's greatest inventor.

Birthday Celebrations

While vacationing in Florida on his winter holidays he was the object of reporters' attention, and although he disliked the press, he sometimes granted interviews in which he made statements on issues, new inventions, and events of the day. Particularly on February 11, his birthday, he gave interviews at a press conference which over the years became institutionalized and included an army of camera people and newsreel photographers.[1]

The Edison family traditionally gathered in Fort Myers on February 11. Karl Grismer, in his *Story of Fort Myers*, writes: "In later years of his life Edison was interviewed by reporters and stories appeared in newspapers throughout the country. It was not until 1928, however, that any public celebration was held and Edison consented to attend a birthday party given by the city to which every school child of the county was invited. Because of Edison's failing health the party was not repeated but in 1931, the year of his death, he marked his birthday by attending the dedication of the new concrete Thomas A. Edison Bridge."[2]

The opening of the new bridge was heralded by a birthday celebration for the "patron saint" of the city. Since Edison was observing his eighty-fourth birthday, the formal ceremonies were kept as brief and simple as possible "in order that the aged inventor may not become fatigued." Mrs. Edison approved the dedication plans, which barred speeches, with the exception of one by Governor Doyle Carlton. The Edison party was escorted to the parade area by a bevy of local high school girls. Highlights of the parade included Seminole Indians from the Everglades, the Trail Blazers, twenty-six local men who in 1923 pioneered the Tamiami Trail through the swamps of south Florida, Harvey Firestone, and many other dignitaries. The star of the show was beloved Mr. Edison, who personally cut the ribbon.[3] In a "Believe It or Not" cartoon in 1935, Robert Ripley pointed out that the Edison Bridge was not illuminated, a condition that was remedied in 1937.[4]

The inventor's birthday was to be commemorated in a more elaborate manner in 1938, when the first Pageant of Light was held.

La Conquista—Edison Festival of Light

In the early days of its settlement, when Fort Myers was a center of the cattle trade, townspeople staged lusty Christmas Day jousts followed by pageantry with a ball, highlighted by the crowning of the Queen of Love and Beauty. Later the celebrations were expanded to a three-day festival in February, La Conquista, or The Conquest of Florida. The event featured the Indian, Spanish, and American phases of Florida history. Activities included boat races, a street parade with marching bands and floats, a carnival, and finally the crowning of a Princess Florida.[5]

Nowhere in America is the memory of Thomas A. Edison so alive as in Fort Myers; here he is considered a patron saint. Elsewhere in the country the image of the Wizard of Electricity has faded and statues and plaques are rusting, but in Florida young and old have always celebrated Edison.

This adulation started in 1914,when the arrival of Edison and his party was eagerly anticipated. That year not only the Edisons but also other notables such as Henry Ford and John Burroughs were expected. A welcoming committee was formed, and the *Fort Myers News Press* reported:

> The committee wishes The Press to earnestly request all Ford auto owners to get busy at once. The machines should be decorated and be in readiness.
>
> The committee that has the welcome festivities is crowded with work and it is up to the citizens to extend general cooperation. It is planned to make this a demonstration that will be notable. . . . It is not only an opportunity to express appreciation of the interest that Thomas A. Edison has ever shown in Fort Myers but also a rare chance to get valuable advertising. —The train comes MONDAY NOON. Get ready! today![6]

For years after the death of Thomas Edison memorial services were held on February 11, the date of his birth. Then one day it was decided that people should rejoice that Edison had lived among them rather than mourn. That is when the Pageant of Light was born.

In 1938 Robert Halgrim, a friend of Edison's, conceived the idea of holding a memorial civic event. Members of the Fort Myers Women's Community Club and the Junior Chamber of Commerce decided to sponsor a spring festival, which they called the Edison Pageant of Light, to be held in conjunction with the memorial service.

The first pageant was a three-day affair during February 10–12, 1938. The celebration included a mammoth street parade with seven bands, fifty floats and stunts, a street carnival, and a Cracker Band contest. The highlight of the festival was a Coronation Ball at which four hundred dancers applauded the crowning of the King and Queen of Edisonia. During her lifetime, the crowning was done by Mina, and thereafter Charles and other members of the Edison family did the honors.

In early years the coronation ceremony and ball were held at the Pier, the Arcade Theatre, and the Civic Center. In succeeding years the events became more and more elaborate: the time was expanded from three days to a week and then to ten days with a magnificent Grand Parade of Light, a glittering spectacle that concluded with fireworks. Since the first pageant, the celebration has been held annually, except for the war years of 1942–45. In

1946 a children's spectacle was added with coronation of a prince and princess and a parade.

Over the years demand for public events increased, and it was not possible to provide enough volunteer leadership to handle all the new activities. Therefore, in 1988 it was decided to turn over the responsibility for the events to a nonprofit corporation. Following the 1989 Edison Pageant of Light, the new organization, the Edison Festival of Light, assumed responsibility for all public events.

Thousands of tourists, home folks, and neighbors stand on the sidewalks in the Florida sunshine in February watching a parade of marchers, orchestras, and floats go by. The spectacular Grand Parade, with more than 130 floats, marching units, and balloons, attracts nearly a quarter of a million visitors to the streets of Fort Myers. In addition to the parade, there are numerous special events, including the All County Middle and High School Band Concert, Mrs. Edison's Hymn Sing, western dancing, concerts, and fireworks at the Fort Myers High School Stadium, gala balls, and shows.

The Edison Winter Home

After the pageant in 1947, Mina Edison stayed on in Fort Myers and, following consultation with her son Charles and Mayor Ralph Kurtz she decided to make a priceless gift. At a ceremony in the Civic Center she donated Seminole Lodge, the grounds, and the laboratory to the city of Fort Myers "to improve and beautify the premises and to maintain them in perpetuity in memory of the grantor's deceased husband." The estate was opened to the public in 1948. In addition to the buildings of Seminole Lodge, the chemical laboratory, and the botanical garden, there is a 7,500-square-foot museum dedicated by Charles Edison. It contains the largest existing collection of memorabilia concerning Edison's inventions as well as the private office of the industrialist and New Jersey chief executive Charles Edison. The collection of phonographs at the museum probably is the most extensive in the world with approximately 170 machines, all in working order.[7]

In 1991 the Edison and the adjacent Ford winter homes were merged and opened to the public.

Notes

CHAPTER 1: MAGNET FLORIDA

1. *Appleton's Illustrated Hand-Book of American Winter Resorts for Tourists and Invalids* (New York: D. Appleton, 1885); *Sea Breeze* (Disston City, Fla.), April 1, 1887.

2. David L. Chandler, *Henry Flagler: The Astonishing Life and Times of the Visionary Robber Baron Who Founded Florida* (New York: Macmillan, 1986); D. Nolan, *Fifty Feet in Paradise: The Booming of Florida* (San Diego: Harcourt Brace Jovanovich, 1984), 81. Plant came to Florida in hope of improving the health of his ailing wife.

3. T. Lutz, *American Nervousness, 1903* (Ithaca: Cornell University Press, 1991).

4. Sidney Lanier, *Florida: Its Scenery, Climate and History* (Philadelphia: J. B. Lippincott, 1875).

5. Peter Martyr, *De Orbe Novo Decades*, in *The Florida Reader: Visions of Paradise*, ed. M. O'Sullivan and J. C. Lane (Sarasota, Fla.: Pineapple Press, 1991).

6. Nolan, *Fifty Feet in Paradise*, 58; C. Freeman, *The Book of Florida Wisdom* (Nashville: Walnut Grove Press, 1995).

7. Lanier, *Florida*.

8. D. C. Miller, *Dark Eden: The Swamp in Nineteenth-Century American Culture* (Cambridge: Cambridge University Press, 1989).

9. John F. Stover, *American Railroads* (Chicago: University of Chicago Press, 1961).

10. G. W. Pettengill, *The Story of the Florida Railroads* (Boston: Baker Library, 1952), 8.

11. E. King, *The Southern States of North America* (London: Blackie and Son, 1875).

12. Matthew Josephson, *Edison* (New York: McGraw-Hill, 1959), 289.

CHAPTER 2: A NEW LIFE

1. L. McGuirk, *The Diary of Thomas A. Edison* (Old Greenwich, Conn., 1972).

2. Mary C. Nerney, *Thomas A. Edison: A Modern Olympian* (New York: Smith and Haas, 1934), 272.

3. *Appleton's Illustrated Hand-Book of American Winter Resorts.*

4. Lanier, *Florida.*

5. G. Holland, "Florida Has Added Five Years to My Life" (interview with Edison), *Suniland* 3, no. 6 (1926): 35.

6. T. A. Gonzalez, *The Caloosahatchee* (1932; facsimile, Fort Myers Beach: Southwest Florida Historical Society, 1982).

7. Information about bamboo in southwest Florida is from Gonzalez, *The Caloosahatchee,* and Naples horticulturist Henry Nehrling, *My Garden in Florida* (Estero, Fla.: American Eagle, 1946). In *A Yank Pioneer in Florida* (Jacksonville: Douglas, 1950), Allen Andrews (of nearby Estero) writes: "It is from the Edison estate that we obtained cuttings of the large bamboos that now grow so thriftily at Estero."

8. F. L. Dyer and T. C. Martin, *Edison: His Life and Inventions* (New York: Harper and Brothers, 1910), 1:308.

9. Patent of W. G. Benedictine for production of palmetto fibers mentioned in *Sea Breeze* (Disston City, Fla.), March 1, 1887.

10. Ledyard Bill, *A Winter in Florida* (New York, 1891); George M. Barbour, *Florida for Tourists, Invalids and Settlers* (New York: D. Appleton, 1882).

11. Harriet Beecher Stowe, *Palmetto-Leaves* (Boston: James R. Osgood, 1873).

12. Holland, "Florida Has Added Five Years to My Life."

CHAPTER 3: FORT MYERS

1. Karl H. Grismer, *The Story of Fort Myers* (Fort Myers Beach: Southwest Florida Historical Society, 1982), 114–16, 157–58.

2. L. H. Marietta, "Excerpts and Chronology of T. A. Edison from the Fort Myers Press and Fort Myers Tropical News, 1885–1931, and Letters from T. A. Edison," Historical Files of the Edison-Ford Winter Estates, Fort Myers.

3. Ibid.

4. T. A. Gonzalez, *The Caloosahatchee*, 81.

5. Marietta, "Excerpts and Chronology."

6. D. D. Runes, ed., *The Diary and Sundry Observations of Thomas Alva Edison* (Boston: Philosophical Library, 1948), 3–38.

7. J. D. Venable, *Out of the Shadow: The Story of Charles Edison* (East Orange, N.J.: Charles Edison Fund, 1978), 256.

8. Marietta, "Excerpts and Chronology."

9. Ibid.

10. Ibid.

11. Ibid.

12. Ibid.

13. Ibid. Mina Edison described what happened on their arrival at Fort Myers and where they spent the first days. According to her, it was at the "Hendry House," although that is probably not correct.

14. W. A. Simonds, *Edison: His Life, His Work, His Genius* (Indianapolis: Bobbs-Merrill, 1934), 244.

15. Marietta, "Excerpts and Chronology."

16. Marietta, "Excerpts and Chronology."

17. M. Smith, *Electric Power: The Florida Handbook* (Tallahassee: Peninsular Publishing Company, 1952).

18. V. Peeples, "Charlotte Harbor Division of the Florida Southern Railroad," *Florida Historical Quarterly* (1972): 291.

19. Marietta, "Excerpts and Chronology."

20. Ibid.

21. Robert Conot, *Thomas A. Edison: A Streak of Luck* (New York: Seaview Books, 1979), 363; N. Baldwin, *Edison: Inventing the Century* (New York: Hyperion, 1995), 260.

22. P. T. Board, *Immokalee, The Murphy-Burroughs Home, 1901* (Fort Myers: Prudy Press, 1992), 2.

23. Marietta, "Excerpts and Chronology."

24. Lawrence E. Will, *Okeechobee: Boats and Skippers* (St. Petersburg: Great Outdoors, 1978), 11.

CHAPTER 4: SEMINOLE LODGE

1. W. T. Neill, *Florida's Seminole Indians* (St. Petersburg: Great Outdoors, 1956), 22.

2. Grismer, *The Story of Fort Myers*, 114–16, 157–58.

3. Venable, *Out of the Shadow*, 254–61.

4. Ibid.

5. Andrews, *A Yank Pioneer in Florida*, 14.

6. *Fort Myers News Press*, January 28, 1904.

7. F. Fritz, *The Unknown Story of World Famous Sanibel and Captiva* (Fort Myers: L. M. Cunningham, 1974), 78.

8. Will, *Okeechobee: Boats and Skippers*, 59–60.

9. S. McIver, *True Tales of the Everglades* (Miami: Florida Flair Books, 1994).

10. Will, *Okeechobee: Boats and Skippers*.

11. McIver, *True Tales of the Everglades*.

12. Will, *Okeechobee: Boats and Skippers*.

13. Ibid.

14. McIver, *True Tales of the Everglades*.

15. K. Hall Proby, *Audubon in Florida* (Coral Gables: University of Miami Press, 1974), 26, 39.

16. W. Garrison, *A Treasury of Florida Tales* (Nashville, 1989).

17. W. Wachhorst, *Thomas Alva Edison: An American Myth* (Cambridge, Mass.: MIT Press, 1981), 39.

18. Andrews, *A Yank Pioneer in Florida*, 15.

19. J. L. Young, *Edison and His Phonograph* (New York, 1890), 15.

20. Mina Edison to Charles and Carolyn, Fort Myers, March 27, 1919, Edison-Ford Winter Estates.

21. *Suniland* 2 (1925): 244.

22. F. Fritz, *Unknown Florida* (Coral Gables: University of Miami Press, 1963), 140.

CHAPTER 5: EDISON'S DISCIPLE HENRY FORD

1. Henry Ford, with S. Crowther, *My Life and Work* (New York: Doubleday, Page, 1924), 234–37; Henry Ford, with S. Crowther, *Edison as I Know Him* (New York: J. J. Little and Ives, 1930), 2–5.

2. M. V. Melosi, *Thomas A. Edison and the Modernization of America* (New York: Harper Collins, 1990), 152.

3. Ibid.

4. Ibid.

5. Pedro Salom, quoted in Byron M. Vanderbilt, *Thomas Edison, Chemist* (Washington, D.C.: American Chemical Society, 1971), 228–29.

6. Letter of Leslie R. Henry, Henry Ford Museum and Greenfield Village, to Thomas A. Edison Winter Home, Fort Myers, February 20, 1969.

7. Robert C. Halgrim, *Tour of the Edison Winter Home Fort Myers, Florida* (Fort Myers, 1957).

8. Ford, *My Life and Work*.

9. John Burroughs, *Leaf and Tendril* (Boston: Houghton Mifflin, 1908), 69.

10. Ford, *My Life and Work*.

11. Kelley E. Burroughs, *John Burroughs: Naturalist* (New York: Exposition Press, 1959), 213.

12. Runes, ed., *The Diary and Sundry Observations of Thomas Alva Edison*, 109.

13. Kelley E. Burroughs, *John Burroughs: Naturalist*.

14. Grismer, *The Story of Fort Myers*.

15. Ford-Edison Office Correspondence, 1914–45, Henry Ford Museum and Greenfield Village.

16. Ibid.

17. Andrews, *A Yank Pioneer in Florida*, 21.

18. Venable, *Out of the Shadow*, 255.

19. Ford-Edison Office Correspondence.

CHAPTER 6: THE GREEN LABORATORY

1. *Fort Myers News Press*, April 19, 1919; J. Beater, *Meet the Author* (St. Petersburg, 1959).

2. Beater, *Meet the Author*.

3. "Reliance," *Fort Myers News Press*, January 28, 1904.

4. Letter of Lewis C. Conant to Henry Ford, October 1944, Henry Ford Museum and Greenfield Village.

5. J. B. McClure, *Edison and His Inventions* (Chicago, 1908), 209–11.

6. R. W. Clark, *Edison: The Man Who Made the Future* (New York, 1977), 227.

7. P. Collier and D. Horowitz, *The Fords: An American Epic* (New York: Summit Books, 1987), 108.

8. R. Lacey, *Ford: The Men and the Machine* (New York: Ballantine Books, 1986), 258.

9. Information about the rescued *Suwanee* is from A. J. Hanna and K. A. Hanna, *Lake Okeechobee: Wellspring of the Everglades* (Indianapolis: Bobbs-Merrill, 1948), 183–84; *Fort Myers Press*, November 22, 1934; and correspondence of A. J. Hanna and Conrad Menge. Information about the reconstruction at Dearborn is from R. Cutler, "Reminiscences," Henry Ford Museum and Greenfield Village.

10. B. M. Bowie, "The Past Is Present in Greenfield Village," *National Geographic* 114 (1958): 96–127.

11. John Burroughs, *Leaf and Tendril*.

12. Mary C. Nerney, *Thomas A. Edison: A Modern Olympian*, 242.

13. Mina Edison, "Notes Taken on Sunday, October 20, 1929, at the Golden Jubilee of Light," Henry Ford Museum and Greenfield Village.

14. Nehrling, *My Garden in Florida*, 1:200.

15. Andrews, *A Yank Pioneer in Florida*, 21; Henry Nehrling, *My Garden in Florida*, 2:98–104.

CHAPTER 7: CAMPING AND TRAMPING

1. T. Lutz, *American Nervousness, 1903*, 90, 94.

2. Ibid.

3. "Thomas A. Edison Automobiling to the South," *Scientific American* (June 1906).

4. Conot, *Thomas A. Edison: A Streak of Luck*, 377.

5. C. Barrus, *John Burroughs: Boy and Man* (Garden City, N.Y.: Doubleday, 1921), 352.

6. Grismer, *The Story of Fort Myers*, 187.

7. Josephson, *Edison*, 458.

8. *New York Times*, February 13, 1914.

9. C. Barrus, *The Life and Letters of John Burroughs* (Boston: Houghton Mifflin, 1925), 202.

10. John Burroughs, *Far and Near* (Boston: Houghton Mifflin, 1904), 262.

11. Barrus, *Life and Letters of John Burroughs*.

12. John Burroughs, *Under the Maples* (Boston: Houghton Mifflin, 1904), 131–32.

13. Picture postcard in the author's possession.

14. John Burroughs, *Under the Maples*.

15. Ibid., 121–22.

16. Ibid., 123.

17. Ibid., 124–25.

18. Ibid.

19. Ibid., 119–20.

20. Baldwin, *Edison: Inventing the Century*, 330–31.

CHAPTER 8: EDISON, NATURE LOVER

1. F. A. Jones, *Thomas Alva Edison: An Intimate Record*, rev. ed. (London: Hodder and Stoughton, 1924), 390.

2. *Suniland* 2 (1925).

3. F. T. Miller, *Thomas A. Edison: Benefactor of Mankind* (Chicago: John C. Winston, 1931), 243.

4. Chamber of Commerce of Southwest Florida.

5. Ibid.

6. Grismer, *The Story of Fort Myers*, 127.

7. George Dock Jr., *Audubon's Birds of America* (New York: Arrowwood Press, 1987).

8. Hanna and Hanna, *Lake Okeechobee: Wellspring of the Everglades*, 341.

9. *St. Petersburg Times*, July 31, 1995, 1, 3.

10. *Birds in Florida* (Tampa: Florida Growers Press, 1951), 86.

11. George Dock Jr., *Audubon's Birds of America* (New York: Arrowood Press, 1987), 52.

12. E. Collin, "The City of Palms," *Suniland* 2, no. 4 (1925): 17–21.

13. Charlton W. Tebeau, *The Story of the Chokoloskee Bay Country* (Miami: University of Miami Press, 1955).

14. M. Derr, *Some Kind of Paradise: A Chronicle of Man and the Land in Florida* (New York: William Morrow, 1989), 138.

15. *Economist,* July 30, 1994.

16. P. Dreyer, *A Gardener Touched with Genius,* rev. ed. (Berkeley: University of California Press, 1985), 150.

17. Ibid.

18. W. C. Cray, *Miles, 1884–1984: A Centennial History* (Englewood Cliffs, N.J.: Prentice-Hall, 1984), 4–10.

19. Nehrling, *My Garden in Florida,* 1:320.

20. John K. Small was not only editor of *The Flora of the Southeastern United States* but also of *From Eden to Sahara: Florida's Tragedy* (Lancaster: Science Press, 1929).

21. R. N. Smith, *An Uncommon Man* (New York: Simon and Schuster, 1984), 403–4.

22. Letters of Mina Edison, November 15, 1912, and March 23, 1920, Edison-Ford Winter Estates.

23. Karl A. Bickel, *The Mangrove Coast,* 2nd ed. (New York: Paschal-Sawyer, 1942), 277.

24. R. Grant, "Tarpon Fishing in Florida, 1889," in *Tarpon Tales, Lost Stories and Research, 1889–1939,* ed. R. W. White and C. F. Baum (Sanibel: Lost Stories, 1990).

25. J. M. Murphy, "Tarpon Fishing in Florida," in *Tales of Old Florida,* ed. F. Oppel and T. Meisel (Secaucus: Castle, 1987), 463–68.

26. G. K. Stoughton, *Tarpon Springs, Florida: The Early Years* (New Port Richey, Fla., 1975), 21–22.

27. T. A. Gonzalez, *The Caloosahatchee,* 112.

28. Venable, *Out of the Shadow,* 257–58.

29. Marietta, "Excerpts and Chronology."

30. Jones, *Thomas Alva Edison: An Intimate Record,* 157ff.

31. Letter of Mina Edison to Charles Edison, April 18, 1920, Edison-Ford Winter Estates.

32. Grismer, *Story of Fort Myers,* 181–82.

33. Hanna and Hanna, *Lake Okeechobee: Wellspring of the Everglades,* 263, 344; G. M. Burnett, *Florida's Past: People and Events That Shaped the State* (Sarasota: Pineapple Press, 1988), 12.

34. Derr, *Some Kind of Paradise,* 159–62.

35. W. B. Meyer, "When Dismal Swamps Became Priceless Wetlands," *American Heritage* 45, no. 3 (1994): 108–16.

36. Interview with Edison, *Suniland* 2 (1925).

37. Andrews, *A Yank Pioneer in Florida*, 490.

38. T. M. Edison, "A Plea for Wilderness," *Florida Naturalist* 35 (1962): 103–4 and 122.

39. Charlton W. Tebeau, *Man in the Everglades* (Coral Gables: University of Miami Press, 1968). Tebeau quotes E. A. Dix and J. M. McGonigle from *Century Magazine*.

40. L. Vance, "May Mann Jennings and Royal Palm State Park," *Florida Historical Quarterly* 55 (1976): 12.

41. James Redford, quoted in J. G. Mitchell, "The Bitter Struggle for a National Park," *American Heritage* 21, no. 3 (1970): 99–108.

42. Edison, Plea for Wilderness.

43. McIver, *True Tales of the Everglades*, 30–35.

44. *Suniland* 2 (1925).

CHAPTER 9: STRANGE SIGHTS

1. John Sedgwick, "Strong but Sensitive," *Atlantic Monthly* 267 (1991): 70–82.

2. *The Romance of Cement* (Boston: Edison Portland Cement Co., 1926).

3. Vanderbilt, *Thomas Edison, Chemist*, 182.

4. F. T. Miller, *Thomas A. Edison: Benefactor of Mankind*, 248.

5. Sedgwick, "Strong but Sensitive."

6. Melosi, *Thomas A. Edison and the Modernization of America*, 119.

7. T. P. Hughes, *American Genesis* (New York: Penguin Books, 1989), 319–23.

8. Marietta, "Excerpts and Chronology."

9. Chandler, *Henry Flagler*, 101–3.

10. Andrews, *A Yank Pioneer in Florida*, 40.

11. Grismer, *The Story of Fort Myers*, 190.

12. John Burroughs, *The Last Harvest* (Boston: Houghton Mifflin, 1922), 243.

13. John Burroughs, *Accepting the Universe* (Boston: Houghton Mifflin, 1921), 259.

14. John Burroughs, *The Summit of the Years* (Boston: Houghton Mifflin, 1913), 217.

15. Rea S. Weber, *The Koreshan Story* (Estero: Guiding Star, 1994).

CHAPTER 10: RUBBER AND GOLDENROD

1. Meadowcraft to Liebold, 1927, Ford-Edison Office Correspondence.

2. A. Lief, *The Firestone Story* (New York: McGraw-Hill, 1951), 149.

3. L. F. Collins, "Rubber Raising," *Hollywood Magazine*, 1924, 8.

4. Vanderbilt, *Thomas Edison, Chemist*.

5. Josephson, *Edison*, 470.

6. Collins, "Rubber Raising."

7. Andrews, *A Yank Pioneer in Florida*, 101.

8. Ford-Edison Office Correspondence.

9. M. L. Coit, *Mr. Baruch* (Boston: Houghton Mifflin, 1957), 120.

10. *New York Times*, March 5, 1927, 7.

11. Simonds, *Edison: His Life, His Work, His Genius*, 316–17.

12. F. A. Jones, *T. A. Edison: 60 Years of an Inventor's Life* (London: Hodder and Stoughton, 1907), 89ff.

13. Marietta, "Excerpts and Chronology."

14. J. G. Growther, *Thomas Alva Edison, 1847–1931* (New York, 1937), 47.

15. Vanderbilt, *Thomas Edison, Chemist*, 293–94.

16. From the Seminole Lodge guest book, March 21, 1929, Edison-Ford Winter Estates.

17. Josephson, *Edison*, 472.

18. H. D. House, *Wild Flowers* (New York: Macmillan, 1961), 292–300.

19. Josephson, *Edison*.

20. James Newton, *Uncommon Friends* (San Diego: Harcourt Brace Jovanovich, 1987), 28, and personal information from an interview with Newton.

21. Marietta, "Excerpts and Chronology."

22. Vanderbilt, *Thomas Edison, Chemist*, 283–84.

23. Lief, *Firestone Story*, 248.

24. Vanderbilt, *Thomas Edison, Chemist*, 305–19.

25. Ibid., 297–99.

CHAPTER 11: SPONGES OF LIFE

1. Thomas A. Edison, "The Mystery of Life" (1920), in Runes, ed., *The Diary and Sundry Observations of Thomas Alva Edison*, 216–32.

2. Clark, *Edison: The Man Who Made the Future*, 107.

3. Ibid.

4. Simonds, *Edison: His Life, His Work, His Genius*, 262.

5. Barrus, *Life and Letters of John Burroughs*.

6. Dreyer, *A Gardener Touched with Genius*, 134, 212.

7. Edison, "Mystery of Life."

8. Ibid.

9. E. Mach, *Conservation of Energy* (Chicago, 1910).

10. Edison, "Mystery of Life."

11. Josephson, *Edison*, 439–40.

12. In his recent biography *Edison: Inventing the Century*, Neal Baldwin aptly summarizes Edison's theories about metaphysical "realms beyond." He obviously was influenced by the German philosopher and mathematician Gottfried Wilhelm von Leibnitz (1646–1716), the Swedish scientist and philosopher Emmanuel Swedenborg (1688–1772), and the English self-educated physicist Michael Faraday

(1791–1867). All these men inspired Edison's thinking in connecting scientific observations with moral and spiritual concepts. His own countrymen and contemporaries, the authors Ralph Waldo Emerson (1803–82), Walt Whitman (1819–92), and their interpreter, Edison's friend John Burroughs, no doubt also fostered Edison's views on nature and immortality.

13. E. B. Wilson, *The Cell in Development and Inheritance* (New York, 1900).

14. Edison, "Mystery of Life."

15. R. W. Clark, *Einstein: The Life and Times* (New York: Avon Books, 1972), 4.

16. Young, *Edison and His Phonograph*, 17.

17. F. T. Miller, *Thomas A. Edison: Benefactor of Mankind*, 293.

18. C. Bode, *The Portable Emerson* (New York: Penguin Books, 1981), xxi.

19. Ibid.

20. Newton, *Uncommon Friends*, 29–30.

21. John Burroughs, *The Breath of Life* (Boston: Houghton Mifflin, 1915), 47–48.

22. John Burroughs, *Accepting the Universe*, 314.

23. John Burroughs, *Breath of Life*, 13–14.

CHAPTER 12: MEDICINE MAN

1. For Edison's view about his own disease and medicine in general, see Conot, *Thomas A. Edison: A Streak of Luck*, 431–33.

2. Simonds, *Edison: His Life, His Work, His Genius*, 258.

3. Ibid.

4. Wachhorst, *Thomas Alva Edison: An American Myth*, 32.

5. Vanderbilt, *Thomas Edison, Chemist*, 6.

6. Simonds, *Edison*, 263.

7. D. A. E. Shepherd, "The Contributions of Alexander Graham Bell and Thomas Alva Edison to Medicine," *Bulletin of the History of Medicine* 51 (1977): 610–16.

8. Ibid.

9. W. H. Shehadi, "Early Use of X-Rays in the United States," *American Journal of Radiology* 161 (1993): 206–7.

10. D. J. DiSantis, "Early American Radiology: The Pioneer Years," *American Journal of Radiology* 147 (1986): 850–53.

11. Newton, *Uncommon Friends*, 21.

12. Conot, *Thomas A. Edison: A Streak of Luck*.

13. Mary C. Nerney, *Thomas A. Edison: A Modern Olympian*, 102.

14. John Burroughs, *The Summit of the Years*, 263–65.

15. Conot, *Thomas A. Edison: A Streak of Luck*.

16. Ibid.

17. Lacey, *Ford: The Men and the Machine*, 237–38.

18. McClure, *Edison and His Inventions*, 81, 87.

19. Ibid.

20. F. T. Miller, *Thomas A. Edison: Benefactor of Mankind*, 81.

21. R. V. Jenkins et al., eds., *The Papers of Thomas A. Edison* (Baltimore, 1981), 1:4.

22. Wachhorst, *Thomas Alva Edison: An American Myth*, 52, 100.

23. Ibid.

24. Venable, *Out of the Shadow*, 116.

25. D. D. DeWeese, *Textbook of Otolaryngology*, 6th ed. (St Louis, 1982); R. F. Gray and M. Hawthorne, *Synopsis of Otolaryngology*, 5th ed. (London, 1992).

26. E. Collin, "There's Only One Florida, Says Thomas A. Edison," *Suniland* 2, no. 3 (1925): 22.

27. Runes, ed. *The Diary and Sundry Observations of Thomas Alva Edison*, 169.

28. Ibid.

29. Newton, *Uncommon Friends*, 12.

30. D. Wright, *Deafness: A Personal Account* (London, 1990).

CHAPTER 13: THE NOBEL PRIZE

1. R. Sohlman and H. Schück, *Nobel, Dynamite and Peace* (New York: Cosmopolitan Book Corp., 1929).

2. Josephson, *Edison*, 276.

3. Excerpts from Nobel committees for physics and chemistry, Royal Academy of Sciences, Stockholm, 1994, personal communication to the author from A. Bárány, secretary of the Nobel committee for physics.

4. Sohlman and Schück, *Nobel*.

5. Ibid.; Clark, *Edison: The Man Who Made the Future*, 159.

6. M. Cheney, *Tesla, Man Out of Time* (New York: Bantam Doubleday Dell, 1981), 195–97.

7. Sohlman and Schück, *Nobel*.

8. Excerpts from Nobel committees, personal communication from A. Bárauy.

9. T. Lewis, *Empire of the Air: The Men Who Made Radio* (New York: Harper Perennial, 1993), 30.

10. Ibid.

11. *New York Times*, October 19, 1931, 27, quoted in Mary C. Nerney, *Thomas A. Edison: A Modern Olympian*, 233.

12. For the college degree, see *St. Petersburg Times*, October 27, 1992.

13. Wachhorst, *Thomas Alva Edison: An American Myth*, 158–59.

CHAPTER 14: GENTLE GIANT

1. Conot, *Thomas A. Edison: A Streak of Luck*, 456.

2. Andrews, *A Yank Pioneer in Florida*, 240–41.

3. Robert C. Halgrim, *The Edison Record* (Fort Myers, 1989).

4. Newton, *Uncommon Friends*.

5. J. E. Gill and B. R. Read, *Born Under the Sun: The Official Florida Bicentennial Commemorative Book* (Hollywood, Fla., 1975).

6. Emil Ludwig, *Of Life and Love* (New York, 1945).

7. Jones, *Thomas Alva Edison: 60 Years of an Inventor's Life*.

8. Wachhorst, *Thomas Alva Edison: An American Myth*, 26.

9. Bickel, *The Mangrove Coast*, 10.

10. Marietta, "Excerpts and Chronology."

11. Ford-Edison Correpondence.

12. *Suniland* 2 (June 1925).

13. Holland, "Florida Has Added Five Years to My Life," *Suniland* 3 (1926).

14. Ford-Edison Correspondence.

CHAPTER 15: WINTER HOMES

1. Newton, *Uncommon Friends*, 22–25.

2. Grismer, *The Story of Fort Myers*.

3. *Tampa Bay History* 9, no. 1 (1987): 32–34.

4. *American Guide Series* (New York: Oxford University Press, 1939), 399.

5. Barnes A. Colcord and Weidenbach N. Colcord, *Early Fort Myers: Tales of Two Sisters* (Punta Gorda: Southwest Florida Historical Society, 1993), 51–59, 76–78.

6. *Fort Myers News Press*, February 21, 1914.

7. Vanderbilt, *Thomas Edison, Chemist*, 133.

Index

awards to, 120–21; birthday party for, 130; and boats, 23, 26–30, 45; and Burroughs, 39, 53–58, 60; cement project of, 77–79; as chairman of Naval Consulting Board, 26, 46, 96, 124; character of, 16, 122–26; children of (*see* Edison, Charles; Edison, Madeleine; Edison, Marion; Edison, Theodore; Edison, Thomas Alva (son); Edison, Will); clash with Ezra Gilliland, 21; deafness of, 83, 93, 112–16; and environment conservation, viii, 59–76, 61–63; experiments of, 43, 87–91, 108; first trip to Gulf of Mexico, 8–11; and fishing, 66–70; health concerns of, 4, 5, 7, 19, 105–16; and Henry Ford, 34–41, 48; interest in fish and fishing, 66, 68–70; interviews with, 19–20, 76, 129–30; inventions of, 6, 10–11, 15, 26–27, 35–36, 44–45, 77–79, 108–10; marriage to Mina Miller, 16 (*see also* Edison, Mina Miller); on molecular biology, 98; myths about, 126–27; nature trips of, 51, 53, 60–61, 70; on nutrition, 111–12; patents of, 92; on pharmaceuticals, 105, 107–8; on pollution, 36; reading preferences of, 11–12;; retirement of, 82; rubber project of, 83–85; on Seminoles, 24–25; spiritual beliefs of, viii, 98–104, 142; on sponges, 96–97; on work, 53; writings of, 77, 106

Edison, Thomas Alva (son), 7, 21–22
Edison, Will, 4, 7
Edison battery, 36. *See also* storage batteries
Edison Botanic Research Corporation, 86
Edison Bridge, 73, 130
egrets, 61–62
Einstein, Albert, 101
electric automobile, 35
electric laboratory, 20

electric therapy, 106–7
electric vehicles, 35–36
electromotive power, 35
Emerson, Ralph Waldo, 2, 102, 142
environmental conservation. *See* conservation, environmental
Evans, James, 13
Everglades, 28, 72, 74
evolution, 103

Faber brothers, 9
facial neuralgia, 107
Fairchild, David, 66
Faraday, Michael, 92, 141–42
Firestone, Harvey, 26, 89; Africa rubber tree project, 86; influence on Edison, 61, 71; and interest in rubber experiments, 85; in Miami, 31, 40
fishing. *See* tarpon fishing
Flagler, Henry, 2, 79
Florida: conservation movement in, 74 (*see also* conservation, environmental); contribution to Edison's life, 127–28; debut of electricity in, 20; health benefits of, 1, 3, 59; myths about, 2; promotion of, 14, 18; springs in, 1, 4; tourism in, 1–4
Florida: Its Scenery, Climate and History (Lanier), 2, 8
Florida East Coast Railway, 4
Florida Federation of Women's Clubs, 74
Florida Internal Improvement Fund, 28
Florida Transit Railroad, 9
Florida Tropical Plant Company, 87
Floweree, Daniel, 21–22
fluoroscope, 109
Ford, Clara, 39
Ford, Edsel, 39, 41
Ford, Henry, 26; Brazil rubber tree project, 86; and Burroughs, 38; and Edison, 34–41, 48; history project of, 46–48; ideas about medicine and food,

ε